The Ultimate
Marketing
Strategy

Become Known as the Expert in Your Field.

Write, Publish and Speak

M.K. Dougherty-Mueller
Cindy A. Fox

This book is meant to guide authors through the process of working with Bootstrap Publishing an author assisted publishing company. It is the work book to the Bootstrap Publishing Classes.

We at Bootstrap Publishing train, speak and provide publishing services in Rochester N.Y. and surrounding areas such as Syracuse, Buffalo, Cortland N.Y. and everywhere between.

We work with many publishing service companies to develop, produce and manufacture books. These companies are represented in this book along with contacts names.

Get extra help and self-publishing tips, secrets, and tricks in these sessions! With decades of experience in publishing, printing, and advertising our passion is getting your book to the finish line. This powerful new workbook familiarizes both seasoned and aspiring authors with every step of the digital publishing process.

Bootstrap Publishing Institute
Mary Kathleen Dougherty
Boot Strap Publishing Seminars/Roc - City Book Publishing Services
Cell: 480-560-4933 or New York 585-342- 0795 **For Class information or 45 Minute free consultations**
mkd@bootstrappublishing.net
www.bootstrappublishing.net

First Edition

Published in the United States of America

This book is meant to guide authors through the process of working with Bootstrap Publishing an author assisted publishing company.

It is the workbook to the Bootstrap Publishing Classes.

Mary's Acknowledgements

To Jerry Racfal retiree of Xerox Corporation who launched, no wait, "tossed" me into the book business in the 90's. Thank you for the tips, encouragement and conversations we had. I miss you.

Valerie Mannix founder of Mercury Print Productions and one of my industry heroes. Thank you for allowing me to test market the world of Print on Demand Book manufacturing that later gave me the technology and know-how to publish and sell over 1000 book titles one book at a time.

Thank you, to my son for his famous one liners that kept me going "one more round." For my positive and beautiful daughter in law, and most of all, my grandchildren Connor and Sydney. For being my motivation and my loves. I will love you forever.

Next to my beloved and best friend and husband Don Mueller, I never believed in destiny till I met you. Thank you for being the wind beneath my wings and always holding me in such high regard. Thank you for providing the support and courage, I will love you forever.

To my dear friend, Steve for believing in me at any stage of the game of life. Your morning conversations gave me the energy to keep going on matter what, and being able to laugh profusely has been great medicine to the soul.

Thank you, Cindy for your patience with my end of this book. Thank you for listening to my sometimes Shenanigans, truly a loyal friend, who taught me that **"nothing happens to me, everything happens for me."**

And last, yet most to God, thank you for the many chances to start over and over, and achieve more each time.

Watch as you instantly become an expert in your field, differentiate yourself from the competition.

Do You Dream to Publish a Book-But Lack the Time or Know-How? Look no further. Learn to publish a book in 30 days. Once you become a published author, friends, family & peers see you in a whole new light!

Cindy's Acknowledgments
Message to My Grandchildren

Miranda, you are my precious gift of joy and excitement. I have the greatest of confidence, that you will lead the way for many young girls who are privileged to witness your bravery to step where you are told to not walk. I have no idea how hard it must be to be a young woman of sixteen in today's society, but I do know you will push closed doors open as I have and you will help other woman complete their dreams as I have, I am so proud of you and so grateful God graced my later years with a granddaughter who will not move mountains but better yet build her own.

Merrick, you are my oldest grandson and although you are just eleven I see a young man of quiet contemplation, one who moves gently with a warm heart capable of loving to the extent of co-dependency. I hope you continue to sing as I have witnessed your brief and talented solos in the last couple of plays I have had the privilege of attending.

Maddox my youngest grandson of seven, you are the rocket ship in the family. The thrill seeker, the jumper, the non-thinker. You are the doer without grace only energy. I see you living an exciting life filled with memories most will never experience, yet enjoy through your powerful stories someday to be told..

I love you all to such a degree you will not be able to comprehend until you are blessed with your own grandchildren. You are my moment, I am your future.

7

When I started as a writer, people used to tell me to write what you know and like. It all sounded simple. But I think it's true: you must write books you feel passionately about.

This book is to show you that you can do anything, no matter how old you are, or how young you are. Anytime, anywhere, and <u>no matter what,</u> you can achieve your highest goals and live your dreams <u>awake.</u>

Self-Publishing Lets Women Break Book Industry's Glass Ceiling.

Virginia Woolf, a groundbreaking author and her own publisher, may have put it best when she declared that "a woman must have money and a room of her own if she is to write fiction." In so few words, she summarized the host of challenges facing female writers.

Many of the issues related to publishing in the days of Virginia Woolf persist. She herself was a self-published author.

We may have made some great strides since then in voting and political rights but, as the wage gap shows, we still have some way to go in publishing.

Female writers like bestselling romance author Nora Roberts are advised by their publishers to use only initials if writing in male dominated genres like suspense, even if they have an established following in other forms of fiction.

Early in her career, even billionaire JK Rowling, was advised to use her initials rather than her first name, to avoid turning off potential male readers.

Self-publishing and independent publishing, through small presses, have become incredibly important for female writers who may not have otherwise been able to reach their audience because of industry gatekeepers.

Female self-published authors have been making the news since Irma S. Rombauer self-published *The Joy of Cooking* in 1931, and, more recently, authors like E.L. James, Amanda Hocking, and Beth Reeks (pen name Beth Reekles).

Author E.L. James' *Fifty Shades of Grey* makes news almost daily. Yet, her sensational best seller was first self-published before a major publisher picked it up. Hocking writes paranormal romances. But she wrote 17 books, and self-published each of them as e-books, before she was picked up by a trade publisher. In 2011, the *Toronto Star* reported <u>Hocking sold 900,000 copies of her books</u> and her annual income was two million dollars.

The story behind many of these female writers echo's the idea that traditional publishing houses didn't have the budget or interest, to bring women on board. And that female authors would not sell books, no matter the content. Female writers turned to self-publishing as the prime avenue to their own self determined success-particularly in the romance category.

Now and Locally

Pittsford resident Michele Piraino, author and registered nurse at the University of Rochester Medical Center, has written and self-published her book *What We Need To Survive*. This is a novel which takes place in Rochester, N.Y. Erica McIntyre lives a privileged life in an affluent suburb of Rochester. Her father is a respected neurosurgeon, and her mother owns a fashionable boutique in the village. The lives of Erica and her mother, Beverly, are changed forever when Dr. McIntyre dies suddenly on the first day of Erica's junior year of high school. On the same day, Erica meets Dwight Washington, an African-American student who transfers to her school as a participant in the Urban-Suburban Program. The connection and universal experiences of the characters keep readers turning pages until the dynamic conclusion of the story.

Michele is now working on the second book of the series, *Hearts Broken*. As the story deepens. the families, friends and colleagues of Erica and Dwight connect in many intriguing ways. Both novels explore complex social issues: Racial and economic disparity, sexuality, abortion, grief, single parenthood, gay marriage, adoption, substance abuse, and domestic violence. These are stories about Rochester, about any small city. These are stories both universal and compelling.

"I've always enjoyed creative writing and hoped to someday write a novel. Patient scenarios and my own life experiences are always swirling around in my head. My characters most often are composites of people...family, friends, and patients that I have met along the way. My writing is a mosaic inspired by my life experiences. Writing has become a therapeutic outlet for managing the stresses and hardships that I have had in my own life. "

Authored by J.A. Goodman

 Accompany Detective Emma Mason and her partner Mitch Delaney track down a psychopathic killer in Rochester NY, as he falls deeper into the abyss of his mental disorder.
Woven into the narrative is a tale of romance between Emma and a wealthy and mysterious suitor, named Peter. Emma struggles when Peter becomes a prime suspect of multiple international crimes, including the murder of his partner in London. The story is rich with investigative science and twists through the streets of Rochester at an invigorating pace, highlighting events which made the city famous. Readers looking for a smart, entertaining mystery will not be disappointed.

About the author:
J. A. Goodman was born and raised in Rochester, New York, and grew up on the shores of Lake Ontario. Writing a novel was a lifelong ambition, but bounced around on the bucket list between life episodes. She married, divorced 13 years later, and raised four unique and independent children. But, while she worked at Eastman Kodak Company as a Quality Control Technician, she refined her writing skills in technical reports, publications and training manuals.

She continued taking technical and creative writing courses at Rochester Institute of Technology (RIT) and Monroe Community College (MCC) until age 47, when she quit her job to attend MCC full time. In 1991 she received an Associate of Applied Science Degree in Marketing with distinction. In 2015, she joined the Osher Lifelong Learning Institute of RIT and began a new journey as an author.

Introduction

A book is the best way to establishing yourself as an authority. Authors are perceived as instant subject matter experts, which can attract media attention, attract clients and prospects, create opportunities for speaking engagements, and more.

If this is on your list of goals this year, move it up to top priority! Holding up a book you have written helps to elevate you as an expert in your field like no other. Become a trusted resource with a published book!

Writing a book can help people. Writing about what you know offers people the ability to learn from your years of experience. If you want to reach a wider audience, write a book. Perhaps you're a coach, a consultant, you own a small business or are in the services arena. By writing even a short book, you can enlarge your area of influence.

Writing a book brings self-gratification. So, publishing books is a wonderful way for your information to get out to the public while giving me a huge amount of self-satisfaction.

Writing a book will give you the confidence to shine in your chosen field.

Writing a book will drive traffic to your website. If you are looking for a great way to get people to your website, then get that book out into the world! Within the pages of any book you write, you have endless possibilities to promote yourself. With an About the Author page you can add information to drive people to your website, other books you've written; the list goes on.

A published book is the best business card ever! I think of my books as a marketing tool for my business. Yes, they are information books and have helped a lot of people write their own books. But they are also the best marketing tool I have at your fingertips.

Write about the subject you know well and are passionate about, and don't let fear be your guide.

Everyone is an expert at something. The problem is that we are unaware of it—or take it for granted. The key is to discover it and step into it. What is your expertise? You aren't doing the world any favors by minimizing your expertise or trying to deny it.

Affirm it.

Once you own your expertise internally, say it out loud:

"I am a writer."

"I am a life coach."

"I am a growth consultant."

Whatever it is, speaking it is the first step in realizing it.

In addition, put it on your business card, your website, and your official bio.

Share it. Your expertise is a gift, given to you for the purpose of sharing with the world. You can express it in a thousand different ways: a blog, a podcast, a speech, an online course, coaching, consulting, or write a book.

Prove it.

Ultimately, the proof of your expertise in in helping others achieve the results they want to achieve. Once this happens, you want to ask for endorsements. Nothing establishes your credibility more than publishing or producing products that flow out of your expertise. Books do this, of course, but so do eBooks, online courses, keynote speeches, and coaching programs.

Why Write a Book

In working with authors over the years, I found that authors write and publish books for different reasons, whether it's sharing their story, inspiring or entertaining others, earning money, and/or promoting their business or cause.

When I asked them here is what they said:
Take your business to the next level
Become more popular (or think you are)
Writing a book can help you conquer fear
Builds inner confidence
Makes you dream bigger
Shifts you to different mind set
Increase your opportunities for adventure
Extend your reach to the world
Go places you've never gone before
Be independent
Process life's experiences
Transform your business
Play on the national/global stage.
Say goodbye to cold calling
Get rid of your cheap customers
Attract nicer customers
Find commonalities with your readers
Great way to position you to charge higher fees
Create additional income streams
Increase your exposure
Build/gain/establish credibility
Launch a new career
Get a promotion
Start/support a consulting business
Prove you are an expert

Tap into your creativity
Help you increase sales
Acts as a powerful business card
Leverage your book to change your future
Create a professional image
Gain recognition
Create value for yourself and others
Separate yourself from the competition
Create a platform with your book and start a speaking career
Expand referral source
Create and sell information products based on your book
Leave a legacy
Realize your ideas
Wonderful and enlightening experience
Work for yourself
Establish, build on a career
A message that needs to be heard
A sense of accomplishment
Express your creativity
Personal expression
Create an image for yourself
Create greater awareness of an issue, a topic
Touch other people's lives
Build a national reputation
Create evergreen marketing for your business
Others become more aware and conscious of you
Help more people
Increase your communication skills
Increase your higher consciousness
Be taken more seriously
Easier to up sell existing customers
People will want to do business with you
Magazine/newspaper interviews
Radio interviews

Television interviews
Attracts like-minded people to you
Challenges you to move forward
Gives you bragging rights
Raises your status
Attracts better opportunities
Gives you a competitive edge
Opens doors
Create a valuable sales tool
Create an evergreen sales tool
Set yourself apart
Builds your name
Have a stronger life purpose
Get traffic from search engines
Writing a book can help you conquer fear
Create fans
Create something out of nothing
Re-visit great events in your life
Re-do events that didn't end so well
Live many lives vicariously
Be productive until you die
Live the life you want on the page
Get your name in the Library of Congress
It's been a dream
Become known, recognized, understood, appreciated
Find your own mythic journey
Stir our spirits
Warm our hearts
Form bridges between people
To mine your own personal gold
Share your gifts
Teach, influence, and bind people together
And because.
And Because It Is On Your Bucket List

To find out what books yours will be competing with, go to Amazon.com and search your book topic.

What titles come up?

Have your read these books?

What will make your book different?

How is your book better?

What gives your book an edge over the others?

When writing a book, it helps to have a solid idea of what you want to cover and who you want to reach.

Let your mind go on this, and brainstorm as many ideas as you can. You may not keep them all, but for now you need to get the material out of your head.

Keep in mind that, at this point, you aren't making any final decisions. Remain flexible and open-minded; you will probably change things around once you start writing and researching.

Making this list will help you get organized and give your writing some direction. The only way to write a book is to sit down and start writing. Dedicate a specific, regular time to write every day. And if you can't write every day, then make sure you write on most days.

While you are writing always be thinking of your reader.

Next write a compelling book description that will motivate your target audiences to buy this book.

Write an engaging author bio. Potential buyers of nonfiction books want to know why they should listen to you – what are your qualifications for teaching them about this topic? Author bios are also important for fiction and children's book authors – they give the reader a sense of who you are. Be sure to make your bio engaging.

Questions

What is your book about?

Do you have pre-written articles that we can use with media and/or excerpts?

What are the three most important things that the reader will take away from your book?

How will this book help the reader?

What is your background, unique qualifications or experience that makes you an expert on the subject of your book?

What are some of your most outstanding accomplishments as they relate to the topic of your book?

What are people always surprised to find out about you or your book?

Tell us about your background, what was the critical "aha" moment that made you decide to write the book?

That was your revelation?

What do you want the book to accomplish for you?

What are major keywords, search terms or search phrases that you use to drive people to your website?

What makes your book thought-provoking?

If you've written other books, what are their titles and who is their publisher?

What are the three most important things that the reader will take away from your book?

Are there groups to which your book would have particular appeal?

List books which cover a similar subject area that might be considered competition for your book.

Are there any well-known people who should see an advance copy of your manuscript for purposes of giving a pre-publication promotional quote? These people do not have to know you personally.

List any people you know personally who might directly give the book added publicity.

List any specialized media that should receive review copies of your finished book?

List any organizations, institutions, or associations that might be interested in either selling or publicizing your book.

Write a few paragraphs on how you came to write this book, including any interesting experiences researching it.

Publishing Options

The Gate Keepers- Traditional Publishing, Publishers Creating Books for a Consumer Readership Publishers acquire, edit, produce, publish and sell the books you're most likely to see in a bricks-and-mortar bookstore.   While there are many trade publishers in the United States, the major ones are referred to as "the Big Five." They are: HarperCollins, Macmillan, The Penguin Group, Random House, and Simon & Schuster.

Textbook Publishers / Educational Publishers / Academic Publishers - Books for Classrooms and Students create books for school and university classrooms, the major textbook publishers are: McGraw-Hill ,Pearson Reed Elsevier, and Houghton Mifflin.

Professional Publishers - Books Geared toward Knowledge Professions
These include (but aren't limited to) accountants, architects, doctors, lawyers and psychologists. Because of the amount of data in these books and the need for constantly updated information, much of this information has moved from predominantly book form to online access. An example of a professional publisher is John Wiley.

Self-publishing/ What this book is about.

Self-publishing is one of the fastest growing segments of the publishing industry. Unlike using traditional publishing companies, self-publishing allows the author to be in control of the entire creative and selling process.

As a self-published author, you might pay the full cost of producing your work and are responsible for marketing and distribution. Therefore, the finished copies, the copyright, all subsidiary rights, and all money received from book sales are exclusively yours.

First-time authors may find it hard to be accepted by a traditional publishing house because of the unpredictable sales of a novice's book. You can test your book's sales potential by self-publishing a small quantity. We provide a full line of services to produce an attractive, professional book, and our many years of experience show the best salesperson for a book is the author.

Traditional publishing companies prefer books that will interest the mass market and will usually not accept a work intended for a small audience Bootstrap Publishing can print quantities of 50 – 5,000 copies very economically so you can publish a book that meets your objectives.

Why Self-publish

Publishing Time — large publishing houses take months to complete your book for sale in book stores. We will complete the finished product in only a few weeks.

Special Interest Books — large publishing houses do not have an interest in special interest books. However, in many cases, books dealing with education, special how-to books, or books on religion have a greater sales appeal to the general public.

Local Interest — large book publishers are not interested in local interest books. However, books with interest in a certain region or community sell very well and can raise thousands of dollars for the author.

Control — you have total control of your book design and where it is sold without dealing with a third party.

Sole Proprietorship — as a self-publisher, you own all rights to the book and are in the position to set your own price with all profits coming to you.

Bigger Profits — if a large publishing house agrees to publish your book, you will get just 3% to 15% royalty on each book sold. As a self-publisher, you can receive 70% to 200% profit.

Family Books — making money is not the only interest of many authors. Telling a family story or just getting their words in print for the next generation is very important.

What Is Assisted Self-Publishing?

Assisted self-publishing is for authors who are tired of waiting around to get published and are ready to shape their own destiny. If you have tried to get your book published with a traditional publisher, but for whatever reason have been unable to do so, assisted self-publishing may be a great option for you. It is also an affordable, efficient option for authors who want more control over their book publishing process than what a traditional publishing house will give you. You remain in control during the entire publishing process.

When you self-publish you only pay for the packages and extra services you want – nothing more, nothing less. Another unique thing about self-publishing that is different from traditional publishers is that you retain all the rights to your book. We do not buy the rights to your book so you are free to continue to market your book to other publishers and outlets at your own pace.

Additionally, when you work with Bootstrap Publishing you will reap the benefits of our earth friendly and state-of-the-art on demand book printing partner. Print-on-Demand technology ensures that you are not left holding a large inventory of books you cannot distribute. We only print a book when it is ordered which cuts down our costs and yours.

It's time for you to experience an affordable, efficient and professional way to publish a book. We are here to walk with you every step of the way, ensuring that all your questions are answered, your book is published to your satisfaction and you receive a book you can be proud of for a lifetime.

Guidelines to Parts of a Book

Books are generally divided into three parts.

The Front Matter

The Body of the Book

The Back Matter.

Title page - is title, subtitle, author, publisher, publisher's location, the year of publication, text, and illustrations.

Copyright page - carries the copyright notice, edition information, publication information, printing history, cataloging data, legal notices, and the books ISBN or identification number.

Credits for design production, editing and illustration are listed on the copyright page.

Dedication - not every book carries a dedication but, for those that do, it follows the copyright page.

Epigraph - an author may wish to include an epigraph - a quotation - near the front of the book.

Table of Contents - this page lists all the chapters, front matter and back matter.

Foreword - contains a short piece written by someone other than the author. The foreword is always signed, with the author's name, place and date.

Preface - the preface tells how the book came into being.

Acknowledgments - the author expresses their gratitude to all who helped in making this book possible.

Introduction - the author explains the purposes and the goals of the book.

Glossary - an alphabetical list of terms.

Bibliography - a systematic list of books or other works such as articles in periodicals, usually used as a list of works that have been cited in the main body of the work, although not necessarily limited to those works.

Index - an alphabetical listing of people, places, events, concepts, and works cited along with page numbers indicating where they can be found within the main body.

Keep these points in mind:

1. <u>Tell the Story</u>: When writing, focus on telling your story. Everything is a story; sometimes there are stories within stories.
2. <u>Let it Flow:</u> When writing, do not worry about spelling, punctuation, neatness. Just write. Write, Write, Write!
3. <u>Write like you speak to find your "VOICE"</u>: Be present when writing and envision a story from your day you want to share with yourself.
4. <u>Practice is the Game</u>: Everything and anything that you want to learn requires practice.
5. <u>Perfectionism</u>: In the field of publishing, editors, copy editors, designers, and proof readers are perfectionists. They clean up your work. Your job is telling the story, teach the method, and entertain your readers.

How to Organize Your Writing:

Once your writing begins to flow, and articles or chapters are starting to pile up, it is important to organize your writing.

If you are writing on a computer, save your writing to a file. I create a file for each book that I am in the process of writing.

I do not write one book at a time, because I usually have several books in process. If you are writing in journals, you'll sooner or later want to take some or all of that material and type it into a WORD Document.

While Writing Your Book

- Name your publishing company. Be careful about using a name that reflects the nature of your book. You may decide to publish books in different genres in the years ahead.

- Apply for a Fictitious Business Name. This is available through your County Clerk.

- Establish a business address. Sign up for a post office box or a box at a mailbox store to use for business correspondence.

- Open a business checking account.

- Request a block of International Standard Book Numbers (ISBN). You will assign one number to each book you publish. This number identifies your publishing company and the book and is necessary for books sold in the retail market. R.R. Bowker is the U.S. agency for distributing ISBN. You will probably want to start with a block of ten numbers, however you can also order blocks of one hundred or one thousand. For more information and to purchase your ISBN printout, visit www.isbn.org. Contact the Agency by phone: 877-310-7333 or email: isbn-san@bowker.com.

- Request an Advanced Book Information (ABI) form. About six months before your book is finished, fill out the form and send it to R.R. Bowker (POB 2068, Oldsmar, FL 34677-0037). This insures that your book will be listed in Books in Print, one of the industry's most important directories. There is no charge for the form or for the listing.

- Request Copyright forms. Contact the U.S. Copyright Office at 202-707-3000 or www.loc.gov/copyright.

Wait to file this form until after you've completed your work on the book.

- Contact your State Board of Equalization and request a resale permit.

Book Writing Template

Title:

Subtitle:

Author:

Foreword by:

For electronic copy: Send for your book template email:
mkd@bootstrappublishing.net

Copyright Page

Here you will print the copyright notice, show the printing history (number of printings and revisions), list the LCCN, the ISBN, the Cataloging-in-Publication Data (CIP), name and address of the publisher and printed in the United States of America or Printed in Canada (to avoid export complications).

Copyright © 2017 by (Your name): First Edition, 2015
Published in the United States of America
Or Canada, UK, Australia, etc.

Dedication page

This is where you, the author, can dedicate your book to readers, family or friends

Epigraph Page

Contains a quotation that sets the tone of the book. Using a separate page for an epigraph is a nice touch.

The Table of Contents

This page will include the chapter numbers, chapter titles and beginning page numbers. You can leave the page numbers out for now. Fill them in later when the book is formatted.

Table of Contents

The Foreword

Try to get an expert in your field to contribute a foreword. Contact one of your peer reviewers about writing your foreword. Help this person by writing it yourself to demonstrate what you are looking for.

Acknowledgments

List everyone who helped you prepare your manuscript and book. People love to see their name in print and each will become a disciple spreading the word about your great contribution to literature.

Disclaimers

....Are showing up in more and more books today. Lawsuits are an unfortunate fact of life and while disclaimers are not absolute protection against them, the warning can't hurt.

The Appendix

......Contains important lists and other resources. Add books, reports, associations, conferences, tapes, suppliers and so on.

The Glossary

is an alphabetically arranged dictionary of terms peculiar to the subject of the book.

The Bibliography

lists the reference materials or sources used in writing the book.

The Index

aids the reader in locating specific information in the pages and is particularly important in reference works. Many librarians will not purchase books without indexes, so plan on including an index. The index is at the very end of the book to make it easy to locate.

The Courage Inside Yourself to Publish a Book

Publishing your first book will take courage. But imagine the accomplishment you will feel when you hold your book in your hands for the first time. Publishing can seem like an overwhelming and daunting, but it doesn't have to be.

Surround yourself with supportive people. This could be your family, the friends you've had since childhood or the group of writers in your community you just met. No matter who they are, make sure they understand your goals and your fears. They should be people who give you positive feedback and cultivate your dream, not tear it down. These should be the people who cheer you on every step of the way, but are candid with you too.

Fear is a dream killer. Fear gets in the way of you achieving your dreams and can cripple you if you don't deal with fear before you even start writing. Be honest with yourself – what are you most fearful of? Once you identify all your fears, write them down, tear up the paper and tell your fears goodbye.

Find the right publishing partner. The best way to achieve success in your writing career is to find the right publishing partner who will walk with you the whole way. Whether you decide to submit your manuscript to a traditional publisher or choose to publish with us, you must be comfortable with your decision.

Tap your inner strength. Possibly you've had an idea for a book in your head for years, or maybe it is a new thought. No matter where you are in the writing process, you will need a healthy dose of your inner strength to help you. Take time to refresh yourself and connect with your inner strength in ways only you know.

During the writing and publishing process there will unavoidably be rough days. There will be moments you want to give up and never publish a book. When those moments come, try your best to stop, take a deep breath and focus on your dream. You can do it!

Traditional and Nontraditional Promotions

Pre-Selling Your Book Before It Is Printed

- Landing Page
- Coupon Data Base Building, Tell everyone you know
- Email Blogs Do What You Do Best
- The EBooks PDF
- Social Networks, meet ups
- Face book, Twitter, LinkedIn

Why They Buy Test Marketing - 20 to 40 Books.

- Associations
- Groups
- Book clubs
- Forewords
- Reviews
- Endorsements
- Awards
- Give a ways
- Agents and Publishers
- Personal Book Signing, Family and friends Sell 50 books break even.

Special Sales

- Airports
- Supermarkets
- Gift shops
- Business
- Schools
- Government

Why They Buy Your Book

- One likes the way your book is presented in an advertisement.
- Someone identified with something about you – maybe they grew up in the same city as you or graduated from the same school.
- Someone the consumer trusts – friend, family, colleague -- recommends it.
- One reads a favorable review of your book.
- The consumer is exposed to media coverage about you and or the book – an article in a newspaper or magazine; an interview on radio or TV; a blog review or interview.
- Someone likes your previous work and/or enjoyed reading a free sample of your new book.
- Someone likes your blog and/or Web site and buys based on that.
- You pushed their emotional buttons and they bought your book out of fear, anger, love, desire, etc.
- Your book appears to deliver solutions to their problems.
- Your book's descriptive catalog or back cover copy draws them in.
- The consumer may like the same charity that you support and bought the book as a showing of solidarity.
- Someone buys it as a gift for another person. Someone needs the information in your book.
- Your author credentials are better than those of authors for competing books.
- Your cover image and title are catchy.

After Publication

Ship and deliver review copies, courtesy copies and pre-publication orders.

Send two copies of the book to the Copyright Office.

Send three copies of the book to the Library of Congress.

Send one copy of the book to Quality Books.

Apply for a business license. Check into your city/county requirements for a business license.

Put your promotional plan into action

Do You Need an Author Website?

 You need a website because someday you're going to send your manuscript to a publisher on the hope that they might be interested. The editor is going to Google your name.

Have you ever googled your name? What comes up?

- Do you want to attract more readers and sell more books?

- Do you want readers and editors to know that you are an expert in your field? If you answered "yes" to any of these questions, you've answered the title question as well: Yes, <u>you need a Web site.</u>

- Worldwide publicity at almost no cost.

- The Internet offers writers an opportunity to promote their books, become more accessible to their readership, establish their expertise, and enhance their professional standing.

- To interact with your readership.

- To educate and inform your readers.

- An introductory home page that indicates the type of articles that will be found on the site. It's a good idea, if possible, to organize a clip site around a particular theme rather than "shot gunning" your site with copies of clips on a host of unrelated topics. Another option is to cluster clips around two or three separate categories (Your home page should also list your name and provide an overview of your credentials.

- Selected clips of your best work. Before posting clips of previously published work, be sure you own the necessary rights. If you've sold all rights, produced the material as work-for-hire, or do not own electronic rights, you won't have the right to put the material on your personal Web site. Nor should you simply scan clips and post them as image files, for two reasons: First, image files are cumbersome to download, and second, a magazine clipping may contain copyrighted elements that don't belong to you (such as artwork, advertising, etc.). If you prefer to scan your clips before posting them, translate them into text files first.

- Copyright information on every page. In your copyright notice, list the title of the material, the copyright date, your name, the name of the publication in which it appeared, and the date of publication.

- A collection of information resources. The best way to establish your expertise is to provide expert information. This could include articles that you've published on your topic, a set of FAQs developed specifically for the site (e.g., "Ten Ways To . . ." or "Questions People Ask About . . ."), or full-length articles written for the site. You might also consider posting a regular column, such as a news column that keeps visitors up to date on developments in your field or a Q and A column in which you answer questions posed by visitors to your site.

- A selection of top-quality links. To position yourself as a vital resource site in your field, you'll need to surf the Web for the best links to other sites in that same field. This accomplishes two purposes: It adds to the value of your site and encourages other sites in the field to link back to you (thereby increasing your traffic).

Remember that your visitors rely on you to screen sites -- don't add any link that you haven't personally checked.

- A bookstore. If your goal is to establish expertise, consider offering a bookstore of titles related to your subject or field. While such a bookstore may compete with your own title, it will also give readers the added benefit of your expert recommendations.

- Your credentials. Keep your bio short, sweet, and professional. Focus on anything that supports your standing as an expert: education, credentials, job history, personal experience, and so on. Let visitors (and editors) know that they can trust you as a source.

- An author bio. Readers will want to know more about you, so satisfy their curiosity with a brief, professional biographical sketch.

- A bibliography. Many authors provide a list of all their writings, including short stories, awards, and any other credits.

- Descriptions of your books. This is your chance to give readers a better summary (and teaser) than they will find on the backs of your books. Try to include images of your book covers as well. If you can't obtain image files from your publisher, you can scan in your covers yourself, or take them to a commercial printer for scanning.

- Background information. Is your book set in a particular historical period, locale, or cultural environment that readers might want to learn more about? Your Web site is an excellent place to answer questions, post background history or details, explain unfamiliar terms and concepts, and provide links to other sources of information on the Web.

- Writing tips. Many of your fans undoubtedly dream of writing the types of books you write. Give them a hand by offering some advice on writing in your field or genre. Such a section will also improve your chances of receiving links from other writers and organizations in your field, because other writers and organizations will regard it as a useful site for writers as well as readers.

- Links. No site is complete without a few links. Choose those that relate to the general purpose and content of your site. Other sources of background information or other sites for writers in your genre. You might also seek reciprocal links with other authors in your field.

- Ordering information. Make sure that visitors can find out where and how to get your books. One easy way to prompt sales is to link your book title(s) to Amazon.com.

What's In Your Book Marketing Tool Kit?

Your best resource to market your book is you. Reach out to the people you know and those that they know.

Your book will get discovered if you market your book utilizing these tools:

- Create a Meetup group
- Increase your web presence:
- Create a testimonial page on your website
- Ask fans to post their reviews on your Facebook page
- Ask fans to post their reviews on Amazon
- Ask fans to post their reviews on Goodreads
- Sign up for Twitter
- Clean up your social footprint
- Create an author FB page and use it instead of your profile
- Sign up for Google Authorship
- Offer bloggers advanced reading copies
- Go on an online book tour
- Create a book launch team
- Host Q+A sessions on Google+
- Create Facebook Friday videos
- Register as an author on Amazon
- Register as an author on Goodreads
- Create a book trailer
- Get a new Author Website

Build your fan base:

- Start a FB campaign to increase your fans
- Start a Google Campaign to increase traffic to your site
- Start a controversial web series
- Link up with other writers for your controversial web series
- Start weekly twitter chats with readers
- Keyword your blog posts
- Create a monthly newsletter
- Create an affiliate program
- Host guest bloggers
- Become a guest blogger
- Create business cards with your web address on them and hand them out
- Put your photo on your business card for stronger branding
- Start commenting on other blogs (early and often)
- Host regular author hangouts on Google+
- Host regular author interviews on Google+
- Record your Google+ hangouts and put them on YouTube
- Get social media coaching

Create an online community with a forum:

- Say thank you to readers with special incentives for being a fan
- Ask your reading community to design merchandise for your store
- Create a fan page for your main character (works well if they are in a series)
- Ask fans to create their own book trailers and post them online
- Offer core fans advanced copy of future books
- Offer "extra features" on your website

- Use Twitter hashtags
- Poll your readers and listen to what they say
- Answer all your blog comments
- Engage with your fans on FB
- Ask your fans to post pictures of them reading your book

Make some extra money:

- Repackage old blog posts and sell them as an e-book
- Join an affiliate program
- Speak on the core topic of your book
- Become a content writer
- Host paid webinars
- Freelance with niche magazines
- Sell ads on your website
- Sell ads in your newsletter
- Write a new eBook tailored to your fans
- Mentor another writer
- Offer customizable eBooks for readers
- Sell your book on your site, not just Amazon

Build your brand offline:

- Write a Press Release
- Ask to be interviewed by your local paper
- Ask to be interviewed by the paper your book is set in
- Ask to be interviewed by the local radio host
- Ask to be interviewed on the local morning show (read this article first)
- Partner with a band that has the same cause as you
- Go on a physical book tour
- Start thinking local
- Rent a billboard
- Host a book release party

- Link with an activity that supports your cause and sell your book there
- Create a viral video about a scene from your book

Find a Place To Give a Book Reading:

- Your local coffee shop
- A hospital
- A retirement community
- A rehabilitation center
- A local church
- A locally owned bookstore
- The library (try the five closest to your house)
- The local community college
- A school
- Wherever the main setting of your book is
- Google+
- Videos you upload to Facebook
- Goodreads
- Women's shelters
- VA hospitals
- Homeless shelters
- Children's hospitals
- Retirement homes
- Host webinars with other experts
- Create a series of web-videos interviewing experts on the core message of your story

Other

- The five closest libraries to your house
- The library in your hometown
- Summer camp
- Community libraries at coffee shops
- The local community college library
- The libraries in the town where the book was set in

- BookCrossing.com
- Prisons
- Church libraries
- Rehab centers
- Cruise ship libraries
- Doctor's offices
- Community centers
- Senior Centers

Content Guidelines

 ***Please take a moment to familiarize yourself with some examples of prohibited content:***

Pornography

Pornography, X-rated movies, home porn, hard-core material that depict graphic sexual acts, and amateur porn are not permitted. Unrated erotic videos and DVDs of the type you'd find at a typical bookstore are permitted for DVD distribution. Any permitted nudity, graphic titles, and descriptions must be sufficiently concealed with censor strips on all items containing such content.

Offensive Material

What we deem offensive is probably about what you would expect. This includes items such as crime-scene videos, videos of cruelty to animals, and extremely disturbing materials. CreateSpace reserves the right to determine the appropriateness of items sold on our site. Also, be aware of cultural differences and sensitivities. Some materials may be acceptable in one country, but unacceptable in another. Please keep in mind our global community of customers.

Illegal Items

Items sold through the CreateSpace service must adhere to all applicable laws. This includes the sale of items by individuals outside the United States. Some items that may not be sold include any products which may lead to the production of an illegal item or illegal activity.

Stolen Goods

If CreateSpace learns that an item is not the property of the seller, or was obtained through illegal means, we will immediately remove the item from our service.

Items that Infringe Upon an Individual's Privacy

CreateSpace holds personal privacy in the highest regard. Therefore, items that infringe upon, or have potential to infringe upon, an individual's privacy are prohibited. Additionally, the sale of marketing lists (bulk e-mail lists, direct-mail marketing lists, etc.) is prohibited.

Recopied Media

Copies, dubs, duplicates, or transfers of music, videos, software, images, etc., are prohibited. Just as you cannot sell a photocopied book without the author's permission, you cannot sell copies or duplicates of videos, music, video games, software, photos, etc. Likewise, you cannot sell transferred media – whether laserdisc to video, CD-ROM to cassette tape, or from the Internet to any digital format--unless explicitly approved by the author.

Movies

Unauthorized copies of movies (VHS, DVD, etc.) may not be sold through CreateSpace. Also, movies that have been transferred from one format to another (unless done by the proper rights holder) are not permitted. For example, NTSC to Pal and Pal to NTSC conversions are not permitted unless done by the proper rights holder. Unreleased/prereleased movies, screeners and trailers are prohibited.

Television Programs

Unauthorized copies of television programs, including pay-per-view events, are prohibited. Commercially produced and licensed copies of television programs are permitted. Unauthorized television programs and unauthorized copies of programs never broadcast, unauthorized scripts, unauthorized props, and screeners are prohibited.

Music

Recopied music in any format is prohibited. Bootlegs, unauthorized live concerts, unauthorized soundboard recordings, unauthorized merchandise, etc., is not permitted. Content containing unlicensed popular music as its soundtrack is not permitted. Likewise, "mix" CDs of unlicensed music are not permitted. Please see our Copyright Guidelines for additional information on rights.

Promotional Media

Movies, CDs, software, etc., that are produced and distributed for promotional use only are prohibited for sale through CreateSpace.

Rights of Publicity

Celebrity images and/or celebrity names cannot be used for commercial purposes without permission of the celebrity or their management. This includes product endorsements and merchandise as well as unauthorized celebrity image collections.

Public Domain and Other Non-Exclusive Content

Some types of content, such as public domain content, may be free to use by anyone, or may be licensed for use by more than one party. We will not accept content that is freely available on the web unless you are the copyright owner of that content. For example, if you received your content from a source that allows you and others to re-distribute it, and the content is freely available on the web, we will not accept it for sale through CreateSpace.

We do accept public domain content, however we may request that you provide proof that your submitted material is actually in the public domain and may choose to not sell a public domain title if its content is undifferentiated or barely differentiated from one or more books already available through our service or available through other retail sites.

Book Reviews

Reviewers are helping you by reading your book and writing a review, whether they like the book or not. They've taken their valuable time to do this, at no pay, out of their love for books.

1. Pick reviewers that review your type or genre of book. Don't waste your time and theirs if they aren't interested in your genre.

2. Ask first. Look at the requirements the reviewers publish on their site and see exactly what they want you to send. These two steps alone will help you get appropriate reviews without delays.

3. When you query the reviewer, offer either the print version or a PDF, or both, since different reviewers will have different requirements.

4. Follow up if you don't hear from the reviewer, but give them a few weeks. Ask if they still plan to review the book.

5. Most of these reviewers do this because they love books. **Appreciate the time and effort they took to write a review.**

James A. Cox
Editor-in-Chief
Midwest Book Review
278 Orchard Drive
Oregon, WI 53575-1129
phone: 1-608-835-7937
e-mail: mbr@execpc.com
e-mail: mwbookrevw@aol.com
http://www.midwestbookreview.com

More

- Create author Facebook and Twitter accounts; add friends and followers.

- Create a website that communicates your personality and what you write.

- Start a blog and post consistently.

- Visit author and agent blogs and comment regularly.

- Create an account on Goodreads. Interact with other writers. Write reviews of their books.

- Join Pinterest. Pin interesting photos (your own to avoid the necessity to request permission to use) that pertain to your work in progress.

- Gather business information for proposal: lists of bookstores, libraries, and churches you will approach to do signings or readings.

- Create a one-sheet to give to editors and agents at conferences.

- Let social media friends and followers know when your book will be published.

- Ask Goodreads readers to review your book.

- Contact bookstores, libraries, and churches on your lists to schedule book signings and readings.

- Prepare sound bite for media that communicates your book's message or story, your brand, and tag line.

- Prepare pitch statement for those to whom you will send review copies.

Why Authors Become Great Speakers

By Cindy A. Fox

Write:

Writers love to write, seems like a fair assumption wouldn't you say? Otherwise why would we do it? Writing is very time consuming, it's very private and it's very intimate. After all we write from the heart, the mind, the past, the future, the pain, the lust, the decay, and the right, the wrong of life itself and most importantly from the simple "need to".

We love to fantasize, create, explore, become, imagine, materialize, laugh, scream, cry, run away, hide, be discovered, lie, cheat, hit, be hit, starve, drowned in our sorrows, live, die, pray and curse. Add the words you feel, think and breath are missing from my list because it's all true. The writer writes from the things most people won't even look at.

I could never write in school. I couldn't comprehend sentence structure or punctuation the very basics of writing. I just couldn't grasp it. It's like my brain cells had a coating of shellac on them and nothing could get in whether I wanted it to or not. I never wrote a book report because I couldn't read well. Comprehension of what I read was a constant struggle.

Today after years of working on my writing and reading skills I've become an avid reader and a hopelessly romantic (want to-be) author. I have volumes of books whispering to each other inside my mind. They're mysteries, self-help, erotica, comedy and even who-done-its. I, as a writer have denied myself the humbling adventure of being an author by not publishing my first book, yes you read right, by not writing. This is my first attempt at putting so many words on paper at any one given time.

Read:

Readers love to read, this we know to be true, no assumptions just a fact. I was told a long time ago if I wanted to become a good writer it was imperative I become a good reader. Not all readers become writers but I believe all writers are readers as well. So I say read, read and read if you really want to become a good writer.

I read only two books that I can remember until I was forty five years old. I can remember reading The Old Man in the Sea and The Pearl at some point in my life.

I truly believe because I read but very little, my life was hindered in my ways. I have come to understand the value of reading and its ability to take us on vacations we cannot afford, fill our hearts with a love we may never experience, enlighten our souls and fire up our hopes and dreams of a better tomorrow. A world without books I pray will never be.

As you read you will find areas where I have repeated myself, trust me it was my intention. Once you find yourself in front of an audience, you will understand why I repeated myself. It's all for you. Enjoy!

Speak:

Speakers love to speak, not always so. Often employees are forced by their employers. Statistics show public speaking it is one of the things humans hate to do. On the other hand if you are a speaker by choice, you love to speak, just like the writer and the reader.

Speaking was out of the question for me.

Are you kidding me, there was no way I was going to get up in front of the class and read or talk for any reason what so ever. I always took an "F" because I knew (you), meaning the class, would make fun of me. I knew (you) would snicker at my cloths, and my hair.

I was a tom/girl and my mother made me wear dresses that had little umbrellas and flying birds on them. She curled my hair in ringlets and I just wanted to die. I hated going to school. I hated my clothes and I hated my hair and truth be known I probably hated my mom for that period of my life. In my home if you didn't like something you were to "suck it up" and be grateful for what you had. Liking it was not important and my opinion never counted. So there was no way on God's green earth I was going to stand in front of the room to suffer more humiliation than I was already dealing with on a daily basis.

I'm here to tell you, today I enjoy writing, I read nearly every day of my life and my favorite thing in the entire world to do is speak before an audience, the bigger the better. My personal best has been before two thousand or so attendees.

So let me see if I can help you work through the horrors of public speaking in the final pages of Mary's wonderful self-help book she has so kindly put together so authors like you can not only write your books but actually sell them and make some serious money.

Aspects of Speaking:

I will cover the general aspects of speaking and offer you simple tools to become great speakers. Hopefully you can glean from my experience and knowledge. I invite you to take what you need, leave the rest and get yourself out there in the public eye. As an author it would be to your advantage to become an interesting, knowledgeable, friendly and hopefully sometimes funny speaker to sell your books.

Once you become a published author you are perceived as an expert in your field. You will be asked to sign your books and sign autographs for those who already have your book and those who cannot afford your book. Yes that's right never refuse to give your autograph even if the person has not bought a thing. Remember when you are in public you are expected to sign your autograph when solicited. Believe me if someone doesn't like you they will not buy another book you have written and that person will be compelled to tell everyone they do not like about you to all who are willing to listen. I'm going to make an assumption here, <u>this you do not want</u>.

Listed next are several benefits of becoming a speaker as well as a published author.

Make yourself available regardless of the size of the event... you want exposure...exposure...exposure and hopefully it is (positive) exposure. There are Writer's Festivals and Conventions to speak at, and a plethora of information on the web.

You will be asked to read your own book aloud... at book launches and author events. If you stutter and stumble on your words, or you cannot deliver with confidence and enthusiasm, your sales could suffer.

As a speaker as well as and author... you will stand out in today's crowded marketplace of authors. Thousands of books are published each week so how do you stand out? If you are a speaker as well as an author, you stand out amongst those authors who prefer to stay out of the limelight. Bookstar.com says, "2013 was called the year of the self-published book as <u>hundreds of thousands</u> marched to the drummer of their own words on their own terms".

Author plus Speaker equals more money... Speakers can earn a speaking fee for a keynote, holding a workshop or seminar that can also increase book sale.

Back of the room sales... Where books are sold as a result of your presentation are guaranteed if you give a great talk, workshop, or seminar.

Being a speaker... affords you a personal connection with more people. When people get to see you in action they get to know you better. Asking you questions allows the audience to connect with you on a more intimate level. Your connection this way is where great marketing is best done.

Word of mouth marketing... is free and most powerful marketing you can use. When your seminar, workshop or speech is memorable your audiences will talk about you to their friends. People will then buy your books, or attend your next workshop or may pass the word on in turn.

A Few Things I Have Come To Know

a) Your audience members will remember you when your talk is entertaining, interesting and memorable.

b) Audiences like simple and easy to understand information. Keep your talk down to earth and clear. The information will be enjoyed as long as it's personal and they can relate to what you are saying. Audiences enjoy a humble honest believable sincere talk.

c) Audiences enjoy a charismatic personality and an easy to listen to voice tone.

d) They look for good energy, conviction, power and passion.

e) Audiences respond to humor and wit, entertainment, tears and other honest emotions.

How to Speak, and Leave a Lasting Positive Memory in the Mind of Your Listeners

Speaking, as is, has a tendency to create a great deal of anxiety because speaking in public generates a very deep fear in many. In other words, the more scared you are the more scared you get. Fear isn't a bad thing for a speaker and certainly has its place when the speaker can channel that fear into enthusiasm, but if it's interfering with how we communicate that fear does become a problem.

There are many levels of communication that gives us different ways of getting our message across especially when we're talking about our book. I will break the problem of public speaking down into understandable concepts for you to digest with the hopes of eliminating some of your misgivings.

Communication:

If your audience does not understand what you're saying you have a problem. One part of the problem is we don't communicate clearly. A lack of understanding or unclear understanding of what we're trying to say causes confusion. For example, if you've written a book about driving a tractor-trailer across - country, sleeping in truck stops, and eating in small town diners you're speaking is going to mimic the language that truck drivers would use.

But now if you're talking to a group of senior citizens and you're telling them how you drove cross-country in your RV, slept at camp sites, ate around an open fire or in your plush kitchen in your RV and you talk as you would to the truck driver, they will not comprehend what you are saying.

So, the point I'm trying to make here is whatever group you're talking to, <u>talk in their language.</u>

I'll never forget the time I went to see, meet and listen to an author whom I had admired for years. This gentleman was a very famous author, he had written many books. I was so excited when I heard he was coming to Syracuse to speak. I bought my ticket, went an hour early so I could sit as close as I could get. I took my seat and waited patiently for this man to grace the stage. He walks on stage, starts talking to us about places where he got his education, told us of things he had done, and shared experiences on his way to the top. His talk was extremely boring, his energy was rather pompous in manor, he used words so big and scientific, he actually talked down to the audience and there was no talk of the subject he had written so many books about. I was extremely disappointed to say the least. I felt ripped off and decided to never go see this author again and to this day I have no desire to read his books any more.

Conversational Speaking:

Public speaking is different than conversational speaking. When you and I sit down to a have conversation we are able to stop and ask questions of each other as we build a rapport. We can offer feedback when needed because the communication is two way. When you're giving a talk or speech your standing before a group of people and they don't have the opportunity to ask questions right away when you make a statement that confuses them. Make your talk clear, hesitate when making a strong point, this gives the audience time to digest what you have just said. I realize a moment of silence can be frightening to many but timing is so very important when giving a talk. Please keep in mind, speaking to a group is not a conversation like you and I would have sitting and enjoying a cup of coffee.

Have you ever heard a speaker talk so much or so fast you became overwhelmed, confused and so ready to leave the building? Or you leave the event knowing you heard great information but you just cannot remember what was said?

If you truly want to make a lasting impression on your audience and encourage them to buy your books without yelling" Hey Buy My Books Will Ya"! Give them time to digest the power words in your talk. What are power words you ask, <u>words that bring forth emotions</u>? Remember, emotions are (energy in motion) they need time to process in the body and mind.

Allow your audience that process and I promise your talk will always be remembered.

I have found the easiest way to open the listen's ear is to open their heart first. Once you have accomplished that your talk will be welcomed.

Pronunciation:

Proper pronunciation is important, if you need to practice certain words go stand in the corner, face the wall and say things like;

- She sells sea shells down by the seashore!
- I slit a sheet, a sheet I slit, a silted sheet I slit!
- Peter Piper picked a peck of pickled peppers... a peck of pickled peppers Peter Piper picked... now if Peter Piper picked a peck of pickled peppers... where's the peck of pickled peppers Peter Piper picked.!

Standing in a corner allows your words to bounce off the wall and directly into your ears. You can also read poetry this same way. Try it you'll see what I mean. Seriously, this is an excellent exercise.

It's great if you have a recorder, you can record yourself because you get to hear yourself. You get to hear yourself articulate the words that you just spoke.

If you get in the habit of speaking sloppy you'll speak sloppy when you're on stage. Speak clearly stay away from big words and slang words, unless they are appropriate.

Emotions:

Please, please, please remember people are driven by their emotions. They remember from their emotions and they buy books from emotions.

I don't know about you, but I know for me, like it or not, I have a tendency to hang on to and remember the negative part of someone's speech.

Once you have spoken in public your fans buy your books because they like you as much as they like your books. Remember, <u>there are thousands of authors writing similar books, make sure they buy yours.</u>

I believe people buy books for several reasons and I believe writers write for several reasons and I believe both are emotionally driven. Simple truth, people buy from emotion. Your talk filled with honestly, enthusiasm and caring for the reader can be the catalyst to sell many books at your presentation <u>and in years to come.</u>

Remember earlier I was telling you about this gentleman I went to see, loved his books but saw him in person and became totally turned off after hearing him speak. I am kind enough to not give you the gentleman's name, but I did share that story with you because I want you to understand the importance of the impact that you have when you speak before a group of people.

You will also know when you're dying on stage. You can feel it from head to toe. Don't panic and never let your audience see you shrinking in your shoes. Stand tall and get them back on your side.

I have used humor to repair broken rapport. Humor can also get you deeper in the hole, so be careful and use gentle/kind humor. I choose humor regarding myself to keep things safe. Learning to laugh at yourself (not in a mean way) but in away the audience can relate to, brings everyone closer.

If nothing works, sometimes it's not what you say or how you say it, sometimes you and your audience are just not a match. The only thing you can do there is be grateful for the experience, leave on a good note and steer away from that particular group of attendees again. It is ok to say no to a speaking engagement. Contact me if you need more guidance in that area. Do not let a bad performance stay in your head. You must own your mistakes, learn by them and get right back in front of the mic again.

Gestures:
Non-verbal points to think about are your gestures. Use subtle gestures unless you are trying to make a certain point that requires extra animation. With gestures, you can place one idea more important than the other by raising one hand and lowering the other. Your hands can enhance your talk and

help guide your listener in gathering clarity about what you're saying or they can distract.

It's also a good idea to not put your hands in your pockets, although occasionally placing one hand into your pocket while crossing the stage can express a note of confidence and relaxation on your part. Just don't jingle keys, coins or any other items you may be storing in your pants. You <u>will</u> start shuffling coins, you <u>will</u> jingle your keys. If it is in your pocket you are going to fiddle with it when you become nervous or unsure of your presentation I promise. Please remember this, empty your pockets I repeat empty your pockets.

It is very unattractive to be standing on stage with items bulging from your clothing whether you are male or female, empty your pockets. If your hands are in your pockets your audience will pick up on your nervousness immediately it's that simple.

If you don't normally talk with your hands when you speak to your family and friends I suggest don't try to use them now. You don't want to look awkward you don't want to look like you're performing. It's important for you to keep your personality, you want the audience to know you. This is a time for you to sell yourself as an author and your book.

For the most part it's important to use modest comfortable gestures in front of you as you speak. Try not to scratch yourself or wipe your nose on your sleeve or pick your teeth when you're at the mic. These gestures seem to disturb some people. Remember you are looking at everyone, more importantly <u>everyone</u> is looking at you. Once you speak before a group, people start buying the author as well as the book.

Engaging:

The most important thing about being in front of your audience, in my opinion, is that your audience must be able to engage with you and you are able to engage with your audience.

If you're busy thinking about where your hands are, what you're doing with your hands and if you're constantly critiquing yourself while standing before your audience they will constantly critique you as well. So if you're comfortable with your hands by your sides or comfortable with your hands as if they were a fig leaf please do so. Make sure your gesture expressions are directly proportional to what you are talking about.

Equipment:

The most general ways of classifying microphones are wireless and wired units. I personally prefer the wireless because I like to move around when I talk. Microphones are also classified by the directional pattern. This is very helpful information for those who need the capability of picking up sound or ignoring sound from specific directions. The most common directional microphone is the cardioid, which picks up sound in mainly a 180-degree half circle. There is also a small spot directly behind the microphone where sound can be picked up.

The uni-directional microphone picks up sound only from one direction, the top and the omnidirectional picks up sound in all directions. While using the uni-directional you have to talk into the top and only the top of the mic. If it has openings along the barrel it is most likely a unidirectional mic. You can position the mic toward you and place it 6/7 inches from your chin. This way the head of the mic can capture the sound of your voice.

The multidirectional mic is the most common type. This mic can and will receive noise from any direction in the room. This means you have to be the loudest sound in the entire room otherwise you risk picking up other sounds that can drowned out your speech. This we do not want to happen. Also bend this mic down and point it 6/7 inches from the chin. Now turn it and point it over your shoulder this gives you the speaker some mobility without interference with your voice. This is the mic that will create feedback if you are positioned to close to the speakers. This can be tested by counting to ten and make sure you use the same tone you will use during your speech.

Let's not forget the lavaliere style mic, looks like a tootsie roll midgie. This is attached to a string tie, simply put the string tie on and cinch it up so the mic is 2 inches below your Adams apple and it also comes as a clip on.

And yes the gooseneck, when using a gooseneck you twist and turn that microphone in different directions simply by taking the gooseneck in your hand and point it toward your chin. Your words will actually carry over into the mic with no problem.

If the mic is to close other noises as well as every "S" that you say will be over emphasized. Believe it or not if you can increase your volume a little bit, stand back an inch or two, from that point your mic will have better quality.

Speaking in a higher pitch voice relieves the stress in your body if you have a tendency to be really nervous as well. This will also help you focus on what you're doing. Actually spending that energy will help you relieve any anxiety you may be feeling. Always rely on the mic and project your voice. Before you know it, you will become so familiar with using the mic and you will start looking forward to the opportunity to speak. It can become addicting believe it or not. Just saying!

Some Recommendations:

It is recommended to check out the room prior to your talk. Now I understand that's not always possible but if it is I encourage you to make that request of your host. I encourage you to exercise a preview if possible the night before your talk because of the personal impact it has on you as a speaker.

Once your mind and body have experienced the room, the unknown (which seems to be the cause of most fears) is lifted and you will automatically become more relaxed when you go to bed and the next day. This visit will invite your mind, as you go to sleep, to visualize your presentation as it will become pre-created. This process allows your body and mind to become familiar with its future surroundings. If for some reason that's impossible try to arrive at the presentation location thirty minutes early, take a look at the room, and get a feel for how it's set up and how the audience is going to be looking at you. Yes I said looking at you.

The lectern should always be on the right side of the stage and the visuals on the left if possible. Everything on the right of the speaker (the speaker's right) is considered positive, everything on the left side of the stage is considered negative.

Years ago, left handed children were believed to be bad, so they were killed and in Christianity Christ sat at the right hand of god. True left handed children are no longer killed and everyone is not Christian but sadly enough people's perceptions can be pretty solid. So, make these adjustments to the room when possible.

Giving Your Speech:

If the room is huge, you may get a sense that nobody's going to hear you when there are 500 people in your audience. Not so, just speak your normal tone and let the mic do the work that is what it is made for.

I can remember doing this one time, when I had the opportunity to speak to a group of 2000 men & women at an outdoor event. As I'm standing at the microphone, looking out over the sea of individuals that appeared to be so far away, I felt I had to speak louder. Wrong...did not need to. The setup people had taken care of any issues ahead of my introduction. I simply asked, in my normal voice if I could be heard by the people in the back row.

It is extremely important to make friends with the microphone. Don't be intimidated. The deal is this, the microphone is designed to make you sound natural and auditable.

Now if neither of these things is happening then the microphone needs to have some adjustment. The most common problem here is either being too close to the microphone or speaking way too loud for the size of the room and the amount of people that are in it. Being too loud or too soft is not good for your audience. Your job is to ensure they enjoy your talk.

Remember you are there for them to observe, understand and enjoy you as the author. Sounds like a lot of responsibilities and it is. But that is the truth of it if you don't want your books stealing the space in your garage become a great speaker.

Here are a couple of things you can do, if there's no one there to do a mic check for you. In advance check with the person in the furthest corner of the room and asked them if they can hear you. Don't be afraid to talk with your audience. Remember you're not trying to call hogs here, you just want to be heard at a level that your audience is comfortable with. Projecting is simply raising your voice slightly so that your tone is natural and so that your audience can hear what you're saying. You do this with your diaphragm not with your vocal cords.

Check the room out you may not need a microphone. Simply using a very nice pleasant tone is your best-case scenario. If you can speak and have everyone hear you without a mic, fantastic that's really the best way to do it. I tell you this because you as an author are more likely to be speaking to small groups at first. So even if you're offered a microphone and you see that there are only 35 or 40 people and there's not a lot of noise around you then I would suggest not using the microphone, just using your voice and be just as pleasant and natural as possible. But of course, if the room is larger if there's a lot of surrounding noise and you feel as though you need the microphone by all means use it.

With a larger audience you get the opportunity to ask your audience if they can hear you. I find that when I involve my audience in some of decision about what's about to take place, they really take some form of ownership and they automatically become more attentive and sympathetic before I'm about to wow their pants off. : -)

I ask you to please think about a couple of things that we really shouldn't do before you start your speech. Don't tap the top of the microphone, don't shake the microphone, don't say testing 12341234 and don't stand real close to the microphone and whisper "can you hear me now". Simply speak into the microphone with your normal speaking voice and ask if everyone can hear you.

Be Aware Of Your Audience:

A speaker must pay attention to what the audience is giving back to them. When you see people in your audience blinking their eyes, their heads falling forward with their chin on their chest, their eyes closed, or when they're head snaps back, eyelids open wide, they wipe the drool from the corners of their mouth and they pretend to be interested in what you just said, guess what, you lost them, they were sleeping or at least trying to. Your talk was probably boring. Yes believe it or not, your talk is in the dumper. Oh well happens to all of us sometime in our career.

A few things could have caused this even if your talk was wonderful. Maybe you spent a great deal of time looking at your notes or maybe your head was down as were reading or you were looking upward if you were searching for divine intervention.

When this happens you actually miss part of your own presentation. It's very important to pay attention to your audience, you want to know where they are, are they with you, do you have their attention. You need to stay aware of your audience. This way you can make the proper adjustments as needed.

One of the ways to make these adjustments is always make eye contact with your audience. Eye contact identifies friends and enemies. As you gaze out over your audience you may find someone who is scrunching their eyebrows. It's important not to be affected by the facial expressions that are negative from your audience members. You have choices here, one you ignore him/her, two you can ask a question, three you can try to figure out what is on their mind or (this is the choice I make) take note of this individual and try to make a personal (one on one) connection after the presentation.

Now if you choose to address the issue at the moment your aware, you can say something like; may I clarify something for you, "I noticed what looked as if you were confused (or whatever expression you saw) by what I just said". At that point the audience member gets to express their issue, and it takes the pressure off you mentally and your ego gets to return to its comfortable zone.

So even if the person's expression had nothing to do you at least you had the opportunity to bring that person back into your presentation energy wise.

You can always misinterpret a person's body language. Just because they're leaning back in their chair their arms are folded and they have a strained look on their face does not mean it's about you. They can be thinking about something that happened yesterday but by addressing it you have the opportunity to check in. It's best to address the person directly by that I don't mean embarrass them simply say something like "sir or madam, do you have a question you'd like to ask"?

Transitions:

Transitions are what hold the presentation together. Transitions allow us to go from one point to another with clarity.

A question transition is used when a difficult subject has come up or when the transition seems to be a big one. Example, ask a question with a show of hands, it is like a magic trick, you have your audience focus on one thing while you are putting together something totally different.

Trigger word. You say the word with emphasis and use that word as the first word of your next statement.

You can see how difficult it could be for someone to accept blah, blah, blah...speaking of acceptance..... See how you have now moved from one subject to another smoothly?

Confidence:

A very wise person told me years and years ago the most attractive person on the planet is not the one who dresses the best, it's not how pretty or handsome you are not how much money is in your bank account, it's not how well educated you are, how much you weigh, what color your skin is, or even how articulate you are, it's about how confident you are.

I promise if you express confidence as you enter the stage and you know what you're talking about your audience will like you. Confidence is expressed through your body language. Body language can make a difference between a successful presentation and a non-successful presentation. Please remember confidence is key to your success as a speaker because 80% of communication is nonverbal.

All about You:

Let's talk about the speaker's body language and facial expressions, this is extremely important. The expression on your face must match the meaning of the words you are saying. Let me say that again, the expression on your face must match the meaning of the words you are saying. If they don't match your audience can become confused and not truly understand what you're trying to say. So if you're happy show it, if you are sad show it. If you are angry look angry, is your frustrated look frustrated. Simply allow your face to communicate your feelings. Honesty is always the best policy. In return your audience will appreciate your honesty. They will respond positively even if they do not agree with you.

Your face leaves a lasting impression. Your face communicates, and it's a big part on your personal trademark. Remember, we remember people by their faces.

When your face pops up in someone's mind you want them to see you smiling not with a grumpy look on your face. Your face is your personal trademark. No one looks exactly like you or smiles like you no one in the universe has your same facial expressions. This allows each of us to have a very personal impact on everyone we encounter. Remember your eyes speaks volumes, so be sincere with your audience, they will eat it up. Your facial and body expressions gives validity to your information.

When speaking to audiences look at everyone in the room. Don't focus on one or two people look at everyone even the people in the back row, the balcony and even in the far corners where you can't even see their faces look in their direction? Occasionally stay fixed on one person briefly, talk directly to them, and then move on. This creates personal contact and the person will feel you spoke directly to them, that's why eye contact is a very very important.

Be passionate and committed to your listeners and to what you're saying, you will shine through even if someone doesn't agree with your point of view.

It is not just your face it is your entire body, remember, everyone is looking at you. Hand and body gestures tell your audience you are actually interested in what you're saying. Believe me if you are not interested in what you are saying your audience will detect that, if you don't care, they won't care. They will not come back. I assume you want them to return and if you are like me you want them to bring their friends with them and their money.

Posture is really important, not only for appearances but more importantly for your ease of breathing which will in turn release the anxiety you may have and your voice will carry a longer distance with greater ease. You will not become fatigued as quickly if your posture is good.

Visual communication is extremely important as we said before. As your audience sits there you must remember one very important thing, you are looking at all of them but they are looking at just you.

Months later after your talk someone will approach you on the street, in a store, at a play or some event, stop you and mention how they were impressed with your talk. You will stand there and wonder who they are.

Never, never, act as if you do not remember someone. Acknowledge their comments and say something like... wonderful, hope to see you again. Be friendly, you are easy to remember, your audience members usually not so much. We want to remember that an audience impression of a speaker is confirmed in the first 3 seconds of seeing you. I have to admit that does not give one much time to be perfect.

So, I say be imperfect because that is who we are. No one is perfect. That's why it's important to stay in a relaxed posture, full height and be proud of yourself, not conceited but proud of yourself. Looking good is impressive.

I certainly do not want to see a speaker with their cloths all wrinkled and look as if they slept in their car all night. You want people to look at you, you want them to listen, and if they are turned off by the way you look they cannot hear a thing you say. I don't care if you have the most important information on the planet they are not going to listen. If you don't care, they won't care.

When you present yourself before your audience it is important to make an entrance with good posture that exudes confidence because that is when they start listening, not when you speak your first words.

Your tone should be enthusiastic so your voice says you would rather be there with them than any place else in the world. Always remember people do not care how much you know they want to know how much you care, and everyone wants to be cared for individually. Everyone wants to feel important. Everyone wants to be your favorite.

How you look is important, if you want your audience to hear what you're saying, to feel what you're saying, to understand what you're saying, I would suggest that you dress conservatively. Dressing appropriately for your audience you are speaking before. By that I mean, if you're before and executive group, attorneys, doctors or CEOs dress in business attire. If you're speaking at a homeless shelter I would suggest you dress down, I don't mean torn jeans and food all over your shirt or blouse; I'm saying casual jeans a nice sweater stay away from the blazer look.

Regardless of the assumed financial status of someone, everyone needs to be treated equally and with respect. If you find you are unable to produce such energy it would be to your advantage, and theirs too, refuse the invitation to speech to such groups. I mean you'll be able to pick up and feel the energy that is being generated back to you from your audience, good or bad.

During Q&A:

When asking your audience for questions and one particular person is attacking or negative, cover their question and move on. Do not select a person from that same cluster of people who are reacting the same way. Take a question from the other side of the room because it is likely their question will be totally different. Look for nonverbal gestures such as arms crossed, someone may roll their eyes, or shake their head no. Steer clear of their questions if possible. Stay relaxed so you can avoid becoming trapped and intimidated. <u>You do not want to lose control of your audience.</u>

Then there is the section of the audience that is leaning forward in their chair, they may be nodding in agreement, and these gestures clearly tell you your message has been received. These gestures make you feel you safe to call on them for questions. When fielding questions choose from various positions in the room just in case you run the risk of group antagonist and choosing from around the room makes a good impression on your listeners. This gives the impression you are being courteous and non-selective.

While a question is being asked nod your head to show you are interested in what they are asking. Make eye contact. If you find yourself not understanding the question don't be afraid to ask the attendee to repeat themselves, you will be surprised because the question will actually be shorter. You repeat the question, asked or paraphrase it to show you have heard and understood what was said. This gives other attendees a chance to hear it if they didn't the first time and it gives you more time to give an answer. And by paraphrasing you get to put a spin on it so you can take back control of the Q&A, if control has been lost. This process makes your talk clearer, easier to understand and more specific. If you do not know the answer do not fake it, do not guess. Own the fact that you do not know and offer to gather that information for the attendee and promise to get that to them... and make sure you get it to them.

Never say you will do something if you won't. This will remove any thoughts of your inability to answer and gives the appearance of your willingness to go the extra mile for someone, someone you don't even know. When answering, answer short and brief, just the facts mam! 30/40 sec should be the longest answer you give. Any longer than that and you are not giving an answer you are giving another speech. Do not... I repeat, do not ask... did I answer your question? Move on to the next, otherwise you can be there all day defending yourself when you had no intention. Don't step into that trap of the hostel questioner.

Then there is the person who actually stands up in the back of the room and their question turns into a dissertation. You must politely interrupt the "speaker" and say "I see you have much to say on this subject, could you give me a specific question". If they start again say, "I understand, but what is your question"? If they continue you can either call on someone else, which I'm not comfortable with or you can offer a solution for example... "I would love to go over that with you but this is not the time, I will gladly give you my email address and you can send me your concern and I will gladly respond, thank you" and point to another attendee on the other side of the room.

Trickster:

Now when you have a trickster in the audience it is important never to repeat their bullshit. You can address this by saying you have made some interesting comments and some of them simply are not true however the answer to your question is bla bla bla. Kill them with kindness. Stand your ground. This is your talk.

You may have a person who asks several questions all at the same time, none of which are related. Ask the person to repeat all of their questions, one at a time. Chances are they will not remember their own questions. Answer one of them and move on.

Interrupter:

Be as polite as possible and move on to something or someone else.

Last But Not Lest...How to End Your Speech:

1. Finish your last sentence, pause and look at your audience all of them, smile softly and say thank you.

2. Thank you for your attention, thank you for your patience, god bless, peace be with you, blessings.

3. Or you can close silently by stop talking, step back from the podium and nod your head.

Any of these ways are appropriate because you have let your audience know you are finish and it is time to applause.

Always accept the applause wait until they are finished saying thank you. If it is a lengthy applause simply lift your head and say thank you. They may not hear you but they will see your mouth move.

There Are Four Major Forms Of Presentations:

Written Manuscript Presentation: A fully scripted speech is the safest form because you never have to remember what you are going to say but you can become very boring very quickly if your head is always down, you show no emotion or animation and you simply read your words. If you do choose this style please, please, please read your speech over several times so you are comfortable with what you are saying. Practice by realigning it paragraph by paragraph and then word by word.

Memorized Presentation: memorizing is another way if you have a photographic memory, no anxiety issues and you love living on the edge. Otherwise I would select a different way to get your point across.

The Heart and Gut Presentation: this is my favorite. You work with no notes, no visual aids, and no nothing. Yes I said nothing... nothing. When done correctly is will offer benefits such as... audience involvement, excellent eye contact, spontaneity of thought and flexibility of words. The only problem with this style of presentation you must know what you are talking about.

Outlined Presentation: you give yourself a few prescript signposts along the way. This form you write down the most important points you want to make and then you improv between these points. This gives your presentation order and allows you to digress and embellish as you go along, just don't digress so far you run out of time and you are unable to get your main points established. These are just models to help you settle on a format. Look at all the pros and cons for each type, select one and get busy putting together your killer talk.

Visual Aids:

Don't use visual aids to eat up time or to take the focus off of you. When putting together your visual aids makes sure you leave enough time for you to talk, this tool is to aid not to be the presentation.
Two reasons to use visual aids, 1) to offer info that maybe too complicated to disrobe 2) for visual impact. Remember a little goes along way.

Visual aids should never, never, never standalone. If there is no need for conversation after the aid, do not use it. Picture visuals are far superior to word visuals. Remember the old saying... a picture is worth a thousand words? Exp. Photographs, charts, diagrams, timelines, maps, computer graphics, BORING. If the visuals will emphasize and support your point then use them. Less wording on the visuals is a plus. You do not want your audience to read, you want them to listen. If you must use words for support on your visual, use no more than 5 lines, no more than 5 words per line.

Always stay close to your visual aid because this establishes an association between you and the visual. A visual aid should never get ahead or behind of your talk.

Do not stand in front of your visual aid. If the area is so large step back so the entire audience can see what you are talking about. They should never have to look through you. Tell your audience what you want them to look at, turn and look at it yourself, point at it with your laser while you are still looking at it and tell your audience what they are looking at, recapture their attention by looking back at them.

It is simple. If you want the audience to look at the screen, you look at the screen. If you want the audience to look at you, you look at them. It is your job to guide them through the visuals.

Flip charts can also be used and seem to do well for small groups. You can create your outline ahead of the presentation and or write on the pad as you present. Minimum letter size should be 3 inches. Here you state your point, write it on the chart and state it again. Abbreviating words is helpful on two points, less for the audience to read and it keeps the focus on you for clarity. You can and will lose their attention if your words are long. It is easier to keep their attention than try to get it back once it is gone. Never give out hand outs before or during your talk unless you want the focus off of you. All handouts should always stand on its own. It is a presentation by its self. If you insist on giving out handouts give them out as they match the screen. Remember visual aids work for you not the other way around.

Let's look at what you are going say. Prepare your presentations, organization is key. One very successful way to capture your audience is to use the Hook-Line-and-Sinker approach.

The hook what is your hook? The hook is a statement that will grab your audience's attention from the get-go. The hook is what is used to engage your listeners. You must get their attention in the first few seconds of your talk. The whole purpose of the hook is to get the audience to stop thinking about what they are thinking about for example; did I turn the coffee pot off, did I put the garage door down, should I go pee or wait till the speaker is finished. You want them to listen to you and forget about everything else.

How to hook;

- Use a dramatic statement, if one pertains to your book.
- Open with a joke if you can tell a joke. If you are not a good joke teller stay away from this hook, your audience will eat you up and spit you out. If you choose to use humor please make sure you select a joke that pertains to your talk.
- Tell a story, but be a good story teller and make it brief.
- Use a lead-in question for example; "Good evening/morning everyone by a show of hands how many people....." Even if they missed the question they will ask their neighbor, WALA! You have everyone engaged.
- Visual hook... if you are using a power point this can be done very easily.

The line...

- What is the main objective of your talk, problem, issue or point of your talk, a sentence or two? This is a general introduction.
- Tell what the components of the main objective of your talk, problem, issue or point are.
- Give them a peak at what you have introduced them to.

The sinker... Tell them what you want them to do, glean, think, or understand. Give a clear message so there is absolutely no confusion to what you have just purposed. Now you have your hook-line-sinker let's move on.

Your entire talk consists of this simple outline...

- Tell them what you are going to tell them
- Tell them
- Tell them what you told them

Preparation: key things that will make your job easier.

1. Assignment, opportunity to give a talk.

2. Who is the group you will be talking to, who else will be speaking, remember... last heard, last remembered. But try to speak first causing the other speakers to rise to your level. Focus on what you are doing, not what the other speaker will do.

Audience analogist is taking the pulse of the group and finding out what makes them tic. Ask more questions.

What do these people do, who's in the group, are they professional people service workers, students? All this makes a difference. Education, age, male, female, mothers, politics, ethnic, do they speak English well?

Find out who is the decision maker, the cheese so to speak, who are your enemies if there should be any, who are your friends, who can you depend on for support.

Try to have a supportive person in the room with you even if you have to bring someone from the outside. If your talk is controversial it is always nice to have someone in your audience that likes you. The purpose of this is to get you to develop a system of preparation. So please feel free to write them down, spend some time reading through your answers

Writing Your Speech

When writing your speech first tell the audience what you want them to know, then tell them something about yourself, this could be about you and your business, your book or whatever you want to plug.

Make your intro an opportunity to market yourself but tell it as if it is conversation and not selling. Tell them of your future interest, this helps to keep the audience engaged and it could lead to you coming back or it may get you a reference outside the room. Remember... <u>people love to buy but they hate to be sold.</u>

Dress for Success:

Dress quietly, I didn't say be invisible, I said quietly.

You want the audience to see you, remember all eyes are on you. Have your cloths pressed and clean.

If you are to eat dinner before your talk and you spill something on your cloths don't try to hide it. Making a humorous comment about it, without blaming anyone, this is a fabulous opportunity to show some humility, it will always work in your favor.

Darker blue cloths and greys for the men, tasteful suites, pants, and dresses for the women and not too much jewelry. Look good.

The exception to all of what I just said is if your persona is eclectic, outrageous, flamboyant or spectacular, if your wear a uniform... wear your uniform. Think about what you are doing.

Donald Trump is known for his hair. Danny Thomas, if you remember him was remembered for his nose. I have gotten more gigs because of some of the shoes I wear.

Take everything into consideration before you step to the mic that's all I'm saying... always be true to you.

Practice your presentation. This can be done in front of a mirror or speak your talk into a recorder and play it back so you know how you sound. Time your talk because you want to make sure your 45 min talk ends at 45 minutes. Check through your visuals if you are going to use any. Double check your spelling if you are going to use words. Realistically one full run through is a good idea. Be comfortable with your information; remember the audience is looking at you as if you are the expert.

<u>Do not practice your talk out load on the very day you are to give it.</u> By this time you need to be ready. By practicing on this day you will start to second guess your abilities and your anxiety level will reach the moon, and all the confidence we have talked about will disappear. Do not discuss any of your information unless you are trying to clarify something for yourself. Always arrive early, at least 30 min, check out the room, the mic, the lectern, sit in the audience and look at where you will be standing on stage. Now check your visual aids. Go to the restroom, check buttons, boogers and food in your teeth and you do not have bad breathe. If you are nervous take a slow deep breath through your nose, hold it for a count of 6 and release it slowly out your mouth with pierced lips till there is no air left in the lungs. Repeat this 3 or 4 times. It will slow your heart rate and quiet your nerves.

Now you're on:

Check how you feel emotionally toward your audience. You need to like them first, show your likeness by genuinely smiling as you enter their attention. You know how you feel when someone smiles fully at you. I have been known to enter the audience and introduce myself to some of the attendees before I start.

Important step, this is where you find yourself, how are you with you. If you are not good with you, the audience will never be good. Don't be afraid to tell yourself you are the best at what you do. Remember that 10 minute standing ovation you got once. Tell yourself how much your past audiences have loved you even if you have to make it up. There is an old saying that has helped many through real though situations "fake it till you make it"

Few Helpful Suggestions:

1. Always start your entrance with the foot closet to the direction you are moving.
2. When possible enter from the (left) negative side of the room, it makes it easier for your audiences to find you.
3. Fold your pages loosely and palm them without leaving any creases. Face your palm toward you so the pages cannot be seen.
Never let the audience see your notes, if they do make sure they only see one page, otherwise they become terrified because it will appear you have an endless speak ahead of them.
3. While the master of ceremony (MC) is reading the intro you wrote for him or her face your audience as you approach the stage.

4. When the MC leaves the podium give him or her time to get settled. Two things happen here, one you are given time to place your pages on the podium and two as the MC settles themselves you get to take a couple of deep breathes before you start and get your notes place on the podium.
Make sure all staples and clips of your pages have been removed and that all pages are numbered.
5. Place the visual aids information in order of importance, top to bottom.
6. Place page one and page two beside each other. When done with page two, slides it on top of page one and so on.

How to Use the Lectern:

First it is a recognized position of authority in the room and whoever is behind it is the recognized leader. Do not clutch, lean on or dance behind the podium unless these actions are used as gestures of relevance. For leaners and clutchers take a half step back. For dancers place your feet shoulder length apart, this will stop the need to dance. It is ok to rest your hands on either side of your pages.

Your Almost There:

If you are going to plant yourself off stage while waiting for the introduction you wrote, pick a place that will not cause confusion or disruption.

Always enter from the left if possible, start with your right foot and face your audience. If you choose to sit in the audience, sit in the front row, never in the middle of the row. Not a good idea to put your fanny in the face of your audience members as you squeeze by them to get to the isle, rude, rude, rude.

When climbing the few stairs to the stage stop on the top step, face the audience and take a slight bow from the waist and then continue to the podium. If you are already on stage, say sitting at a banquet of chairs and tables have your notes in a manila envelope, do not put them on the lectern early because the MC may pick them up and take your notes with them after your introduction. While you are waiting for the intro open your chair so you are facing the current speaker and slide your notes out of the envelope. This way when you are introduced you will avoid getting your feet caught on the chair legs and your entrance is cleaner.

Room Set Up and You

Room set up using round tables is not my first choice because the audience is going to have to turn their bodies and become uncomfortable physically during your talk. If your audience is uncomfortable, they are less likely to pay attention. Flat floor presentation is done on the same level as your audience. Main point to remember here is to make sure your audience can see you. With a small room, say up to 15-18 people, put the seating in a u-shape and you stand at the opening. If you are at a conference table, try to stand at the end and present standing. Standing gives you and your listeners a sense of authority. A semi-circle is good for 30 or so people. This allows you to make eye contact with everyone in the room. Over 30 choose the auditorium style and always... always stager the chairs so you are visible to all attendees. With this set up your ability to walk around and get close up with your audience is good.

Seating arrangements plays a huge part in your success as a speaker. If you have any say in the matter leave this selection as a last resort.

Usually food and drink are part of the evening when speaking at a banquet or convention. Do not drink before your speech. Alcohol slows down the mental processes. Don't use alcohol as an excuse to calm your nerves, that's an excuse, not a reason.

Personally, I prefer not to eat before a speech. If you feel you must eat, eat lightly. It is always best to have protein before you speak and avoid deserts, sugar will thicken your saliva.

It doesn't hurt to have a small mirror with you to check the food particles that have decided to make a home between your teeth. If there is time you can always excuse yourself to go to the bathroom to do a last minute check before the big mirrors.

It is a good idea to bring an extra copy of your introduction to the event because the MC has a tendency to lose things. Oh yes, remember where your napkin is. You don't want to stand with it tucked in somewhere on your body. Be sure you did not tuck the table cloth in your waste and not your napkin.

The Media

Why is this important? <u>Who controls the message controls the game</u>. Watch the show a few times before you are to be a quest. Get a feel for way the interviewer works. Who is your audience? What time of day is the show on, who watches it? Offer a bio, ask, who will you be sharing your time with, are you the only guest speaker?

You must know how to play to the camera. You want the interviewer to like you if possible. I'm certainly more forgiving with someone I like. Build a rapport with reporters and editors. Remember you may give an interview but if it isn't live and most of the time it isn't, your words can be manipulated when on film and tape. Be respectful of the media and hopefully they will be respectful of you. I'll never forget the time I was miss quoted, it nearly cost me my job. I would never accept an interview from that reporter again. It wasn't that he didn't like me, he didn't like the company I worked for and he took advantage of my interview, twisted it and made my employer look terrible. So it can help to make up a list of questions that might be asked or you can ask the host for a copy of their questions.

Caution, when you are in front of the camera you is going to be created by the media, for the media. Don't be afraid to ask yourself and the media why you are being asked to appear. How long is the segment? Take some business info if you think it could help your interviewer. Who owns the station can even be interesting information if your material is controversial.

Is this show live or taped, is there an audience in the studio? Where is the taping, when and what time do I arrive? Never assume anything...ever. Just know that the more personal and difficult the questions will be asked.

Practice if you can, be clean, wear solid colors, and avoid white and little jewelry. Always accept the makeup and be kind to the artist, remember they are an artist. Let your face reveal your enthusiasm. Look at the host unless otherwise directed. Keep your ego in check. If you become mad you are dead in the water.

Go watch other speakers, this is one of the best ways to see what you want to be like and not.

A Few Great Authors Who Also Are Speakers:

Maya Angelo gained her recognition for her first book and bestseller... I know why the caged bird sings. This book sold over two million copies in 1970. Her messages are inspiring and her voice is pleasant to hear. She speaks all over the United States.

Mr. Less brown is also an author and speaker. Mr. Les brown as a speaker and author has designed coaching programs for corporate leaders and sports leader's and entertainers all over the world. He had no formal education yet Mr. Brown's passion to learn has given him world recognition for his books and speeches.

Jack Canfield is a motivational speaker and author. Jack Canfield, one of my personal favorites has authored nearly 200 books in 40 different languages and remembers, his first book was self-published. These people made and so can you.

This could be you!
If I can help in any way you can contact me at
315-560-6361
cindyfox@shesunlimited.com
www.shesunlimited.com

In the beginning some publishing houses may have owned and run their own printing presses, but not always. Now most publishers hire printing companies who specialize in printing books to do the printing. The publisher is like a general contractor, who finds the talent, manages the intellectual property and creates the final copy of the work in preparation for the printing; and then of course provides the marketing and distribution to bookstores. This of course, takes a large investment of time, money, and other resources.

Publishing houses like to find authors who already have an established fan base so their investment is assured of a quick return of their investment.

Mary K Dougherty, With more than 24 years of experience in the business of publishing. She can help you make smart decisions about your publishing and digital media strategy, and position you for long-term growth.

Since 1998, She has spoken at hundreds of venues, including writing conferences, seminars, classes, and creative writing programs. She offers thought-provoking and educational talks to audiences of writers and other creative professionals.

Mary K. Dougherty's Consulting has helped scores of authors avoid the pitfalls of self-publishing. She works with a team of designers, copywriter, webmaster, photographers that will take your book from manuscript to print. Mary also can advise you on the creation of support materials and services to launch the title and author, on who to use for distribution and fulfillment, and what it means to start your own independent press.

She has developed original seminars and an entirely new type of marketing technique to break through publishing barriers that typically that offered high powered solutions to self-publishing authors -get books printed affordably 100 at a time vs. the major investment of printing high volume offset print runs.

Through Bootstrap's techniques, now authors print their books as they promote in national bookstore chains and media AND sell them at a profit margin. A sensation has begun. "Print to Promote - Promote to Print" business and marketing model skyrocketed. With so many authors wanting to "get the word out"--Bootstrap expanded to keep up with authors who need cost effective printing techniques--proven marketing methods--and a coaching process that has launched 100's of Bootstrap authors to lucrative careers.

Mary, as founder, visionary and owner behind an author-driven success story that has grown into not one--but three businesses: Bootstrap Publishing, Express Success Test Marketing, and Cover to Cover Seminars.

For the past sixteen years, Dougherty has been a frontrunner in the fast-paced industry getting authors words from print--to book format--but more importantly--how to launch that product successfully into a highly competitive marketplace.

Mary:

I consult one-on-one with authors, small businesses, and publishers. If you have questions about the publishing industry, the self-publishing landscape, I can cut through the confusion, provide concrete next steps, and offer trusted resources. I'll help you understand the service landscape and which services are best for you to use. I hand hold you through the process, from concept to distribution. I'll share resources of trusted freelancers to help you edit, design, and format your work.

Cindy A. Fox

In 1994 I left my job at Niagara Mohawk to go into business for myself. This decision was prompted by my daughter's suicide that took place on Dec. 17 of 1993. Although I had a very good paying position and wonderful benefits with the company it no longer met my needs. I needed to take my daughter's horrific act and create something useful out of it, and this was purely out of survival. So she's Unlimited became a means for my healing as well as my financial security.

She's Unlimited consists of my traveling and speaking at colleges, churches, agencies, etc. on the topics of self-esteem and self-worth. Since that time the company has grown in a consistent positive direction.

Using her own unique, entertaining and engaging style, Cindy Fox, a veteran of the Speaking and Seminar circuit offers fun filled, jam-packed, educational and inspirational seminars meant to awaken the vast potential inherent in everyone's spirit.

With a refreshing approach, Cindy demonstrates methods geared for a rapidly changing and challenging world - going beyond the masks of habit forming, stale patterns of thought to an open environment where new ideas and lives have the opportunity to grow and prosper.

Cindy's timely and purposeful seminars cater to the increasing number of people who are open and ready for new tools and resources to better prepare their mind, spirit and body for "Beyond Your Wildest Dreams".

The Art of Thinking

Is Cindy's latest workshop. This workshop takes "people past their past" using the holistic approach to excellence, creates results no other workshop can produce. During our time together the clients are able to Identify, Heal and Reclaim themselves. The process is quick, simple and life changing. Three of the many results are, Improved health, relationships be it work, family or romantic, take on a whole new life and people are able to gain control in areas they never dreamed possible. Remember thinking is not a science, it's a learned behavior. You too can learn to have the life you have always dreamed of.

Congratulations!

You have just taken your first step toward writing and publishing your book.

Thank you for the opportunity to help you get your book idea out of your head and into the world, where it can bless others and earn you the recognition, prestige, and income that comes from being a published and successful author.

Please feel free to call me if you have questions or exciting things around the book happening I love to hear the evolution of a great work.

Your cheerleader

Mary Kathleen Dougherty
Boot Strap Publishing Seminars/Roc - City Book Publishing Services Cell: Arizona 480-560-4933 or New York 585-342-0795 For Class information or 45 Minuit free consultations mkd@bootstrappublishing.net
www.bootstrappublishing.net

Intent to Self-Publish Agreement

I, Name) _____,
hereby make an agreement and <u>commitment to and myself</u>
that I am planning to publish my book
by_____ (date).

Promise with Self: In making this agreement, I understand the primary goal is to publish my works, thoughts, quotes, photos, illustrations, concepts, ideas, (known as creative material) as part of the process of understanding the print on demand method for sharing creative works with myself, others and/or the marketplace.

Completion: I understand and agree that launching a creative work and to bringing it through all of its stages from conception to completion is the most important part of becoming a self-published author. I promise myself, my publishing coach, and any other students in the course (if participating in a course) that I will finish, no matter what, no matter how polished or "unpolished," imperfect, or flawed I may perceive the work to be.

Challenges: I also understand there may be breakdowns, challenges, fears, anxieties, obstacles, and insecurities in this process of sharing some of the most inspirational and vulnerable parts of myself when I chose to become a published author. I agree that I will continue to move without delay through those difficult spots, knowing that when I finish and publish that <u>I will become a more developed writer, artist, and person.</u>

I understand the choice to become a published author begins a journey which may open many new doors for me, and that this is an inner journey as well as an external one.

I agree to organize no more than 2 focus group meetings of select friends, experts, and advisors for initial feedback on cover and interior design. Afterwards, I will not allow "random, opinionated, or endless changes and corrections" of my book cover, or interior content, from "too many cooks in the kitchen." In harmony with the professional and experienced advice of my publishing coach, and with timeline in mind, I take control and accept responsibility for decisions involved in the self-publishing process.

Patience with Self: Finally, I agree to be patient and allow myself to grow, learn, and expand into a better version of myself during this process. I agree to hold myself responsible and accountable for that, and will read all the material and do all my homework according the publishing schedule. Therefore, I expect the best possible outcome.

Signed:

_____

Date_____

WITNESS:

_____

Date_____

Testimonies

"Mary is very committed to helping speakers, authors and coaches get their message out into the world. Her enthusiasm, creativity and commitment are delightful to behold! Blessings, Karen Rev. Karen Russo, author, The Money Keys, ww.TheMoneyKeys.com"

Mary at Bootstrappublishing.net "Mary is a hard-working dedicated professional. She is creative, well organized, and has always developed and maintained superb working relations with business partners and clients alike. The care and concern for the needs of clients are reflected in her spectacular work."

Jerri Ann Peters, Licensed Marriage and Family Therapist, Orange County Rescue Mission – Village of Hope worked with Mary at Bootstrappublishing.net "Mary knows her industry. Knowledgeable about the publishing business and how to go about getting someone published. Great at making a business plan and following through to completion." Personable, Expert, High Integrity.

Sam Joy, hired Mary as a Publishing "Mary has successfully published hundreds of books for a multitude of clients across the country. She has the knowledge and experience to make every project a success and is extraordinarily pleasant to work with."

Sara White, Publicity and Promotions director, CJM Books was with another company when working with Mary at Bootstrappublishing.net "Mary was extremely valuable in providing guidance on our writing project not only for self-publication but also for marketing and promotion. Thank you Mary!" Top qualities: Great Results, Personable, Expert.

Michael Thaub, hired Mary as a Business Consultant   Mary helped me compile and evaluate book publishing and promotion alternatives. She suggested many ideas but also listened to me and help me sort through the alternatives that were individualized to my background, assets, and needs. This was very helpful and resulted in an optimized result that suited my needs rather than a "one size fits all" approach. Her knowledge of book publishing was a great help in evaluating the alternatives together. I rate her A+." Personable, Expert, and Creative

Bob Shane brook, hired Mary as a Writer/Editor
"I couldn't have self-published my first novel without Mary's help. She helped me pick the right editor and helped to design my book's cover. I had so many questions about the process, and she broke it all down for me to make sense out of.

More importantly, after the book was finished, she was able to help me get the book in the right hands for publication. Now, I'm working on novel #2 and will turn to Mary again for the finishing touches." Top qualities: Personable, Expert, and Creative

"Ms. Dougherty hosted, MCed, and played and integral part in the planning and execution of our brainchild, Rochester's 1st annual Publish Your Book Retreat, (bookretreat.org). Without Mary's commitment, creative contributions, and savvy media relations, the retreat might have fallen on its face. Instead, our event was an enormous success, and the authors who attended are still seeing results today. I plan on working with her again in the future, and for anyone who wants to self-publish, her expertise and market-tested strategies are invaluable."

Chris Murphy, Founder & Executive Project Manager, CJM Books was with another company when working with Mary at Bootstrappublishing.net "Mary is a very energetic and dedicated worker. She is able to bring out the best in clients. I would feel very comfortable recommending Mary.

"Dale, Owner, Lady Be Fit Express was with another company when working with Mary at Bootstrappublishing.net "Mary is a woman of integrity and you may safely expect that all that she says that she will provide for you she will do

Judy Azar LeBlanc, hired Mary as a Writer/Editor in "Mary provides a unique service to writers that are much needed in today's competitive publishing environment." Personable, Expert, and Creative

Claire Gurus, hired Mary as a publishing in "Mary is inspirational when working with authors. I got lots of valuable ideas from working with her and she helped me believe in myself and my work. I recommend her services to all writers who need an expert in the field." Great Results, Personable, Creative

Mary Fachman, hired Mary as a Business Consultant in "Mary is more dedicated to her career than anyone I know. She simply gets out there and does it no matter what it is. She inspires people to believe that "they can" be it write a book, be an artist, start their own business, whatever she intuitively sees in them that needs Karen Hewitt, Owner, Realty Connection was with another company when working with Mary at Boot Strap Publishing "Mary is dedicated and passionate about everything she does! Her boundless energy and enthusiasm translate into excellence in her work. Mary is also a genuinely nice person. She makes doing business a pleasure."

Michelle Nichols, Owner, Practical Training Solutions LLC was with another company when working with Mary at Boot Strap Publishing "Mary was very helpful in getting my book self-published."

Heather Kirk , Owner and Graphic Designer, PhotoGraphic Artistry and Publishing was with another company when working with Mary at Boot Strap Publishing "Mary showed up in our life when I was looking for someone to help publish our book, "When I Awaken, Soul Passages.' Being a first time author we were green and Mary's patience and assistance helped us to put together our book with ease and grace. She is dedicated and has a positive approach to her work. I would recommend her highly.
Respectfully,

Shirley Catanzaro, hired Mary as a Writer/Editor "Mary and I have worked together, her knowledge and experience in self-publishing and her willingness to share that information and experience is astounding. Any aspiring author would be hard pressed to find someone better suited than Mary to mentor their manuscript into being!"

Mike Bercaw, VP Operations / Owner, Sir Speedy Scottsdale was a consultant or contractor to Mary at Boot Strap Publishing "I have had the privilege of working with Mary a few different times. I have found Mary to be a true expert in the self-publishing industry and a valued team player. Mary has brought new ideas to me and helped me to get them initiated into our corporate culture. Personable, Expert, High Integrity

David Clair, hired Mary as a Business Consultant in 2009, and hired Mary more than once "Mary is the consummate professional and really understands her business. More importantly, she understands her clients' needs, wants and aspirations and helps them achieve their goals. Mary is someone you want to have in your corner."

"Mary is easy to work with, knowledgeable of the process, has great suggestions for improving the finished product, and is cost effective. Wish she were here....we are publishing our 5th book without her! Top qualities: Personable, High Integrity, Creative

Don Wells and Jean Groen" Don and Jean, hired Mary as a Shepherded our book from writing to printing in 2003, and hired Mary more than once "Mary knows the ins and outs of the publishing world, her knowledge is valuable to any author seeking help with publishing their book."

Keep 100% of your rights

The intellectual property and copyright of your book is very valuable. You should always retain all your rights.

Keep 100% of your royalties

Make more money by setting your own pricing! Only with Bootstrap Publishing can you set your own retail price, author discount, and Price Plan. You receive 100% of your author royalties.

Unlimited wholesale and retail availability

Bootstrap Publishing books are available for order through online retail sales channels like Amazon, Barnes & Noble, Borders, and more. Plus, with our amazing distribution-on-demand your book can be available for order from just about anywhere that sells books. This means you receive unlimited wholesale distribution through Ingram, Baker & Taylor, and more. Regardless of how many books you sell via wholesale channels, we'll produce the inventory to fill those orders, without any out-of-pocket printing costs for you.

Bootstrap Publishing Your Self-Published Book.

Free Publishing Class AND Free How to Book "Is Writing a Book on Your Bucket List" and Free 45 Min. Consultation

All Publishing Logistics

Packaging- Cover and Lay out

National and International Distribution

EBook Publishing and EBook Distribution

Mini Webpage (Landing Page Advertisement)

10 to 15 Books and 500 Book Marks

And Hand hold you through the Writing and Publishing Process

Guidance in tracking your sales and reordering your printed books.

Promotional and Marketing Plans Suggestions.

Call for Pricing,

A List of Book Genres

Fiction Genre List

- Action and Adventure,
- Chick Lit,
- Children's,
- Commercial Fiction,
- Contemporary,
- Crime,
- Erotica,
- Family Saga,
- Fantasy,
- Dark Fantasy (probably still a major sub-genre!)
- Gay and Lesbian,
- General Fiction,
- Graphic Novels,
- Historical Fiction,
- Horror,
- Humor,
- Literary Fiction,
- Military and Espionage,
- Multicultural,
- Mystery,
- Offbeat or Quirky,
- Picture Books,

- Inspirational,
- Romance,
- Science Fiction,
- Short Story Collections,
- Thrillers and Suspense,
- Western,
- Women's Fiction,
- Young Adult.

Non-Fiction Genre List

- Art & Photography,
- Biography & Memoirs,
- Business & Finance,
- Celebrity & Pop Culture,
- Music, Film & Entertainment,
- Cookbooks,
- Cultural/Social Issues,
- Current Affairs & Politics,
- Food & Lifestyle,
- Gardening,
- Gay & Lesbian,
- General Non-Fiction,
- History & Military,
- Home Decorating & Design,
- How To,

- Humor & Gift Books,

- Journalism,

- Juvenile,

- Medical, Health & Fitness,

- Multicultural,

- Narrative,

- Nature & Ecology,

- Parenting,

- Pets,

- Psychology,

- Reference,

- Relationship & Dating,

- Religion & Spirituality,

- Science & Technology,

- Self-Help,

- Sports,

- Travel,

- True Adventure & True Crime,

- Women's Issues

I am still looking for writers or authors just like you who has something to share with the rest of the world- something that would inspire or motivate people to move on or go on further...who has something to share that is encouraging or could be an eye-opener to the rest is what we are looking for. I am sure that with what you are writing, you could be a hero to somebody. Share your thoughts so the rest of the world would relate and would gain confidence through you!

As you know, once you commit and make the decision to move forward – powerful forces and energies set into motion to propel you to your goal.

Now show the world what's inside of you!!!
We are giving a 45 min. free consultation.

Simply put, there are not many things that seem to bring as much credibility as a well-written and marketed book.

People just look at you differently (in a good way) when you're a published author.

We are proud to represent a very diverse group of authors.

<u>Our Roster Of Authors Includes</u>: Wellness Physicians, Correspondents Professors And Teachers From Universities, High-Schools, Quantum Physics, Recluses, Coaches And Consultants, Advertising Executives, Fairies And Their Friends , Science Fiction & Fantasy and their Friends, Clergy From Many Religious And Spiritual Associations, How-To Specialists , Not –For- Profit Fundraising, Mediums And Intuits, Poets And Eccentric Grandmas And Innovated Mothers, Even Kids Publishing For Kids.

Writer resource list

1 http://annerallen.blogspot.com – One of Writer's Digest's 101 Best Websites for Writers, Ann updates on Sundays and her blog includes regular contributions from former Big Six editor, Ruth Harris.

2 http://www.booksandsuch.com/blog/ – Books and Such is a Literary Management Agency. They sell books to a wide range of publishers in such categories as women's fiction, general fiction, nonfiction, gift books, easy readers, and chapter books.

3 http://goinswriter.com/ – Jeff Goins started his blog in 2010, with a few burning questions in mind: How do successful writers make a living? What does it really take to get published? And, how do you pursue a passion? He shares tips on writing, creativity and making a difference.

4 http://writetodone.com – Mary Jaksch, Chief Editor, believes your writing practice needs to be directed in a positive way. Write to Done helps you learn new skills, practice them and become a better writer.

5 http://jodyhedlund.blogspot.com– Jody posts on her blog every Tuesday. She offers advice, encouragement, and inspiration based on all that she's learned about writing, publication, and marketing in today's tough publishing industry.

7 http://www.helpingwritersbecomeauthors.com – K.M. Weiland mentors authors through her blog. Her blog is one of Writer's Digest's 101 Best Websites for Writers.

8 http://www.trainingauthors.com – Shelley and Heather of Training Authors have a goal to help authors achieve book marketing success. Their site is full of resources and free downloads.

9 http://davidgaughran.wordpress.com – David Gaughran focuses on how to get visible and sell more books. He has written several books on these topics and shares tons of info about self-publishing.

10 http://www.rachellegardner.com – Rachelle is a Literary Agent for Books and Such. She started her blog as a way to create a community of writers both published and seeking publication.

12 http://www.sellingbooks.com – Cathy Stucker shares useful tips and techniques for writing, publishing and selling books. She has free downloads available to help authors build their platform.

13 http://www.selfpublishingreview.com/category/blog/ – Offers review and editing services. You can become a member for additional perks and discounts.

15 http://catherineryanhoward.com/ – Catherine writes from Ireland and talks a lot about self-publishing. Her posts are fun and informative.

16 http://blog.writingspirit.com/– Julie Isaac, the founder of has provided tools, solutions, and support to thousands of writers since 2003.

17 http://marketingchristianbooks.wordpress.com/ – If you've written a Christian book, Sarah Bolme offers guidance on marketing within that market.

18 http://socialmediajustforwriters.com/ – Frances Caballo shares tips and suggestions for using social media to your advantage to market your work.

19 http://louisem.com/– Louise Myers talks all about the power of social media graphics, and offers tips on how you can make your presence more visually appealing.

20 http://writerunboxed.com/ – Writer Unboxed has articles from a ton of contributors that all offer advice and food for thought on the craft and business of writing fiction.

21 http://www.hughhowey.com/ – An author himself, Hugh doesn't just use his site to promote his own work, he uses it to help other authors as well.

22 http://www.thecreativepenn.com/blog/ – The Creative Penn is packed with information and resources. The best way to navigate through it all is to click on the "Start here!" link.

24 http://booklife.com/ – Publishers Weekly's new site dedicated to indie authors, is in Beta mode. They have how-to stories and author profiles, and you can take one of their publishing self-evaluations.

25 http://www.norulesjustwrite.com/blog/ -CJ Lyons is a pediatric ER doctor turned NY Times bestselling author. He uses experiences and offers wonderful resources for the self-published author.

26 http://jakonrath.blogspot.com– JA Konrath is an author who blogs a lot about current events in publishing and on topics that authors should familiarize themselves with.

28 http://www.lindsayburoker.com – A Fantasy author herself, Lindsay doesn't just promote her own work on her website. She also promotes other authors AND writes blog posts with helpful advice on self-publishing.

29 http://www.thefutureofink.com – The Future of Ink has a lot of content directed at helping authors navigate their marketing choices. Denise Wakeman and Ellen Britt have pulled together a huge list of experts and great articles. Don't miss this one!

30 http://indiereader.com – Everything about indie authors, books and the independent book scene all in one spot.

40 Questions to Ask Yourself About Your Author Platform

From Create Space Blog

The key is to ask yourself the right questions. Using targeted self-publishing questions, you can evaluate yourself on what you still need to accomplish to become a more successful author.

Have you set up an Author Central account on all the different language Amazon stores?

Is your author page optimized with a picture, description, Twitter profile, and a video?
Have you edited your book descriptions with the same precision as your books?
Is your description compelling?
Is it over 300 words so it can be properly indexed in search engines?
Does it include your keywords?
Do your book covers fit your genre?
What would it take to make your covers fit in with your category's bestsellers?
If you write in a series, do your covers reflect that in their branding?
Are your keywords optimized to either get you into a new category or increase your search rankings on Amazon?

Have you applied those optimized keywords to the other retailers?

Does your book's front matter and back matter link to your email list?

Would the offer you're making to sign up be compelling enough for you to click through if you saw it in another author's book?

If not, how can you spice it up?

How do you keep in touch with your readers?

Would you classify them as excited to hear from you?

How could you increase that excitement further?

How do you connect with new readers?

Is your website optimized to attract and accept new readers?

What could you do to make your site more inviting?

Where do your readers hang out?

Do you have a presence on those platforms?

What could you do to make sure your time there is well-spent?

Who are the biggest authors in your genre?

What are they doing that makes them so successful?

Have you ever reached out to any of them for advice?

What do you think they would tell you to do first and foremost?

How much time do you spend on marketing per week?

How much of that time leads to quantifiable results?

What are some ways you could make your marketing more efficient right away?

Is your catalogue selling as well as it should?
Why or why not?
What are five steps you could take to make your books sell better?
Is your writing time as efficient as it could be?
What about your writing process?
What could you do to streamline both to create more work more effectively?
What are the most important lessons you've learned this year about running a better author business?
What's holding you back from applying those lessons?
How will you overcome those roadblocks?

> Image from
> http://168opportunities.com/you-are-a-writer-podcast/

How much money have you invested in your author business?
If you had more to spend, then what would you use it on?
What would you need to do to save enough money to pull that off?
What do you think is the best possible publishing path for you in the next year?
How about the next five years?
What goals would you have to set in the next few months to start down that path?
How will you learn to become a better writer?
What kind of skill level would you like to attain in your lifetime?
What might you need to do to reach those heights?

How hard are you willing to work to make your career a success?

How can you best set yourself up for success in the years to come?

Setting your intentions

- What are 1–5 experiences you want to have in 2017

- What are 1–3 relationships you want to focus on deepening in 2017

- What are 1–3 ways I'd like to get out of my comfort zone in 2017

- What are 1–3 ways I want to show care and love to myself in 2017

- How do I want to be feeling exactly a year from now

- What is the word or phrase for my year in 2017

Book Review Magazine Editors and Reviewers

Book Review Magazines

AudioFile, Robin Whitten, Editor, 37 Silver Street, P.O. Box 109, Portland ME 04112-0109; 207-774-7563; Fax: 207-775-3744. Email: info@audiofilemagazine.com. Web: http://www.audiofilemagazine.com. Motto: The magazine for people who love audiobooks. A bimonthly magazine covering the world of audiobooks.

The Believer - featured here: http://magagenie.com/the-believer

Blackberry Express, Toni Trent Parker, Editor, Kids Cultural Books, 65 High Ridge Road #407, Stamford CT 06905; 203-359-6925; Fax: 203-359-3226. Email: bbg@blackbooksgalore.com. Web: http://www.blackbooksgalore.com. A quarterly newsletter on African-American literature for children.

BlackBoard Bi-Weekly, Carr' Mel Ford White, Editor-in-Chief, 5361 Refugeee Road, Columbus OH 43232. A biweekly newsletter that became a stand-alone publication in June 2001. It features stories and reviews involving books for African-Americans.

The Bloomsbury Review, Marilyn Auer, Editor-in-Chief, Owaissa Communications, 1553 Platte Street #206, Denver CO 80202-1167; 303-455-3123; Fax: 303-455-7039. Email: editors@bloomsburyreview.com. Web: http://www.bloomsburyreview.com. Bimonthly book review magazine.

Books & Culture: A Christian Book Review, John Wilson, Editor, 465 Gundersen Drive, Carol Stream IL 60188; 630-260-6200; Fax: 630-260-0114. This bimonthly magazine reviews books on science, politics, culture, fiction, etc. from a Christian perspective. Circulation: 16,000.

BookForum, 350 Seventh Avenue, New York NY 10001; 212-475-4000; Fax: 212-529-1257. Web: http://www.bookforum.net. A quarterly book review publication with a focus on literary fiction, serious nonfiction, and photo/art books.

Chris Lehmann and Michael Miller, Editors

Albert Mobilio, Fiction Editor

David O'Neill, Assistant Editor

Alfredo Perez, BookForum.com Editor

Book Links: Connecting Books, Librarys, and Classrooms, Laura Tillotson, Editor, American Library Association, 50 E. Huron Street, Chicago IL 60611-2729; 312-944-6780; 800-545-2433; Fax: 312-337-6787. Email: ltillotson@ala.org. Web: http://www.ala.org/BookLinks. This magazine is designed for teachers, librarians, library media specialists, booksellers, parents, and other adults interested in connecting children with books. It publishes bibliographies (book roundups), author profiles, and other articles.

Booklist, American Library Association, 50 E. Huron Street, Chicago IL 60611-2729; 312-944-6780; 800-545-2433; Fax: 312-337-6787. Web: http://www.ala.org and http://www.booklistonline.com. Published twice monthly. Of the 30,000 adult books they receive each year, they review about 4,000.

Brad Hooper, Editor, Books for Adults. Email: bhooper@ala.org.

Donna Seaman, Editor, Books for Adults. Email: dseaman@ala.org.

Laura Tillotson, Editorial Director, Books for Youth. Email: ltillotson@ala.org.

Ilene Cooper, Children's Books Editor. Email: icooper@ala.org.

Gillian Engberg, Young Adult Book Editor. Email: gengberg@ala.org.

Sue-Ellen Beauregard, Editor, Audiovisual Media. Email: sbeaureg@ala.org.

Rebecca Cnuk, Reference Book Editor (Reference Books Bulletin). Email: rvnuk@ala.org.

Galleys or other prepublicaton copies of reference books (dictionaries, encyclopedias, etc.) may be sent, but two finished copies are required before a review can be published. Titles will not be reviewed more than six months past their publication date.

Bookmarks, Jon Phillips, Editor and Publisher, 1818 MLK Boulevard #181, Chapel Hill NC 27514; 888-356-8107. Email: letters@bookmarksmagazine.com. Web: http://www.bookmarksmagazine.com. A bimonthly magazine featuring reviews of novels and a few memoirs, biographies, and current event essays. Their content is excerpted from book reviews printed in various newspapers and magazines.

BookPage, ProMotion Inc., 2143 Belcourt Avenue, Nashville TN 37212; 615-292-8926; Fax: 615-292-8249. Web: http://www.bookpage.com. This monthly tabloid review is distributed in hundreds of bookstores. We do not give review consideration to self-published books, print-on-demand titles or books from presses that lack major distribution.

Lynn Green, Editor

Abby Plesser, Fiction Editor

Kate Pritchard, Nonfiction Editor

Allison Hammond, Children's Editor

Bookreporter, The Book Report, 250 West 57th Street #1228, New York NY 10107. Web: http://www.bookreporter.com. "The majority of our reviews on Bookreporter.com are fiction. We review bestsellers, contemporary fiction, classic fiction, debut authors, mysteries, thrillers, some science fiction, and some romance. We also delve into nonfiction, newsworthy books, biographies and memoirs." There are several genres they generally do not review: how-to, self-help, health/medical, spiritual, religion, and travel guides. Also no ebooks, POD books, or self-published titles without wide distribution.

Tom Donadio, Editorial Manager. Email: tom@bookreporter.com.

John Hogan, Contributing Editor, Graphic Novels and Manga. Email: john@bookreporter.com.

Bulletin of the Center for Children's Books, Deborah Stevenson, Editor, 501 E. Daniel Street, Champaign IL 61820; 217-244-0324; Fax: 217-244-3302. Email: bccb@illinois.edu. Web: http://bccb.lis.illinois.edu. Reviews more than 900 new children's books per year in 11 issues. Only trade and mass-market books are considered. They don't review textbooks, curricular materials, audios, videos, software, electronic publications, or magazines.

Catholic Library World, Catholic Library Association, 100 North Street #224, Pittsfield MA 01201-5178; 413-443-2262. Email: cla@cathla.org. Web: http://www.cathla.org. Quarterly magazine for Catholic schools, libraries, etc. Send books for review to the address above. They review books on theology, spirituality, Catholic religion, pastoral, and Catholic books for children and young adults (12/10).

Sigrid Kelsey, General Editor, 141 Middleton Library, LSU Libraries, Baton Rouge LA 70803; 225-578-2720. Email: skelsey@lsu.edu.

Choice, 100 Riverview Center, Middletown CT 06457; 860-347-6933; Fax: 860-704-0465. Email: submissions@ala-choice.org. Web: http://www.ala.org/acrl/choice. Published by the Association of College and Research Libraries, they publish nearly 7,000 reviews per year (about 25% of the books they receive each year). Their focus is on books, tapes, e-books, etc. appropriate for libraries that serve students at the undergraduate level, including community colleges. Also selective graduate level material of interest to advanced undergraduates. No undergraduate texts, foreign-language material, reprints, or professional texts. For more information and submission deadlines, contact Barbara May via email: bmay@ala-choice.org.

Context, ISU Campus 8905, Normal, IL 61790-8905; 309-438-7555; Fax: 309-438-7422. Email: context@centerforbookculture.org. Web: http://www.readcontext.org. This quarterly publication primarily focuses on literary fiction, poetry, and cultural studies. They also publish a sister review publication, The

Review of Contemporary Fiction, with a focus on fiction (email: rcf@dalkeyarchive.com).

Curtis White, Editor

Tim Feeney, Book Review Editor

Design Book Review, Richard Ingersoll, Editor, 1418 Spring Way, Berkeley CA 94708; 510-486-1956; Fax: 510-644-3938.

ForeWord Reviews - http://magagenie.com/foreword-reviews

Horn Book Magazine, 56 Roland Street #200, Boston MA 02129; 617-628-0225; 800-325-1170, ext. 4; Fax: 617-628-0882. Email: magazine@hbook.com. Web: http://www.hbook.com. For submissions information, go to: http://www.hbook.com/booksubmissions.html (5/09).

Roger Sutton, Editor. Email: roger@hbook.com.

January Magazine, #101-1001 W Broadway #192, Vancouver, British Columbia V6H 4E4, Canada. Email: editor@januarymagazine.com. Web: http://www.januarymagazine.com. This online magazine reviews fiction, crime fiction, children's books, art & culture and cookbooks. They've featured interviews with Joseph Epstein, Ruth Ozeki, Russell Rowland, John Shannon, Sylvia Fraser, Russell Banks, Joe Sacco, Janice Galloway, Lee Child, John Connolly, Gabor Mate, Rohinton Mistry, and others. They do interviews, profiles, some news, and book reviews.

Linda Richards, Editor. Email: linda@januarymagazine.com.

J. Kingston Pierce, Crime Fiction Editor. Email: jpwrites@wordcuts.org.

David Middleton, Art and Culture Editor. Email: david@januarymagazine.com.

Kirkus Reviews, 1133 Broadway #406, New York NY 10010; 212-209-1531. Web: http://www.kirkusreviews.com. Submission guidelines: http://www.kirkusreviews.com/about/submission-guidlines (be sure to read these guidelines!). This publication reviews more than 500 pre-publication books every month: fiction, nonfiction, childen's books, and young adult books (1/11).

Eric Liebetrau, Managing Editor and Nonfiction Editor, 479 Old Carolina Court, Mount Pleasant SC 29464; 843-754-3784. Email: eliebetrau@kirkusreviews.com.

Elaine Szewczyk, Fiction Editor; ext. 25. Email: eszewczyk@kirkusreviews.com.

Vicky Smith, Children's & YA Editor, 99 Mitchell Road, South Portland ME 04106; 207-671-6846. Email: vicky.smith@kirkusreviews.com.

Perry Crowe, Discoveries Editor; ext. 22. Email: discoveries@kirkusreviews.com. Self-published books and books that have already been published. You must pay for these reviews.

Molly Brown, Senior Online Feature Editor; ext. 20. Email: molly.brown@kirkusreviews.com.

Lambda Book Report, Greg Herren, Editor, Lambda Literary Foundation, P.O. Box 73910, Washington DC 20056-3910; 202-682-0952; Fax: 202-682-0955. Email: lbreditor@lambdalit.org. Web: http://www.lambdalit.org. Monthly book review of gay/lesbian books.

Library Journal, 160 Varick Street, 11th Floor, New York NY 10013; 646-380-0700; Fax: 646-380-0756. Email: ljinfo@mediasourceinc.com. Web: http://www.libraryjournal.com. Book review submission

guidelines:
http://www.libraryjournal.com/csp/cms/sites/LJ/SubmitToLJ/TitlesForReview.csp Monthly book review journal aimed at librarians.

When submitting books for review, include the following information: Author, title; name, address, and telephone number of publisher; date of publication; price; number of pages; and ISBN and LC numbers if available. Please indicate whether any illustrations, an index, or bibliography will be included; also include a brief description of the book, its intended audience, and information on the author's background.

We prefer to receive materials three to four months in advance of publication date since our primary goal is prepublication review. We will accept galleys, page proofs, or manuscripts (only one copy is necessary). Those publishers (small houses) that cannot supply advance galleys may submit finished books, but these should be sent as early as possible with the words "In lieu of galleys" and the publication date affixed to the cover.

Francine Fialkoff, Editor-in-Chief; 646-380-0715. Email: ffialkoff@mediasourceinc.com.

Michael Kelley, Executive Editor, Features & News; 646-380-0740. Email: mkelley@mediasourceinc.com.

Barbara Hoffert, Editor, Prepub Alert; 646-380-0726. Email: bhoffert@mediasourceinc.com.

Heather McCormack, Reviews Editor; 646-380-0736. Email: hmccormack@mediasourceinc.com. Also Graphic Novels Review Editor.

Wilda Williams, Fiction Editor; 646-380-0755. Email: wwilliams@mediasourceinc.com.

Margaret Heilbrun, Senior Editor; 646-380-0723. Email: mheilbrun@mediasourceinc.com.

Michael Rogers, Media Editor; 646-380-0744. Email: mrogers@mediasourceinc.com. Reviews audiobooks in CD, mp3, and other formats. Promotional material must accompany each audiobook, noting publication date, number of discs, number of hours, whether abridged/unabridged, narrator, category, ISBN, and price. Please also specify whether an MP3-CD and/or digital downloadable edition is available.

Bette-Lee Fox, Video Review Editor; 646-380-0717. Email: blfox@mediasourceinc.com.

Henrietta Thornton-Verma, Reference Editor; 646-380-0748. Email: hthornton@mediasourceinc.com.

Anna Katterjohn, Magazines Editor; 646-380-0729. Email: akatterjohn@mediasourceinc.com.

Cheryl LaGuardia, Online Database Reviewer. Email: claguard@fas.harvard.edu. Also writes the E-Views blog.

Josh Hadro, Associate Editor, Reference & Academic Newswire; 646-380-0722. Email: jhadro@mediasourceinc.com. Also Online Database Reviewer.

At the ALA Conference in 2001, Hoffert reported that out of the 600 to 900 review copies she receives each week, she sends out 10 to 20 for review (but they actually review more than 6,000 books each year, which works out to about 120 books being sent out for review each week).

The Big Five Trade Book Publishers

Hachette Book Group

Hachette Book Group (HBG) is a division of the second largest trade and educational book publisher in the world, Hachette Livre which is based in France and is a subsidiary of the French media company, Lagardère.

Hachette's American roots trace back to 1837 when one of its publishers, Little, Brown and Company, was founded. Time Warner acquired Little, Brown in 1968 and HBG was created when Hachette Livre acquired Time Warner Book Group in 2006.

Hachette's publishing divisions include: Grand Central Publishing; Little, Brown and Company; Little, Brown and Company Books for Young Readers; Faith Words; Center Street; Orbit; Yen Press; Hachette Audio; and Hachette Digital.

237 Park Avenue

New York, NY 10017

(212)364-1200

hachettebookgroup.com

HarperCollins

HarperCollins Publishers is a subsidiary of News Corp, the global media company led by Rupert Murdoch.

The "Harper" half of HarperCollins began in New York City in 1817 as J. and J. Harper, named after its founders, brothers James and John Harper. It became Harper & Brothers and, eventually, Harper & Row, which NewsCorp acquired in 1987. In 1990, NewsCorp acquired the British publisher William Collins & Sons and formed the worldwide book group.

Some of HarperCollins publishers and imprints are: HaperCollins; William Morrow; Avon Books; Broadside Books; Harper Business; HarperCollinsChildrens; HarperTeen; Ecco Books; It Books; Newmarket Press; Harper One; Harper Voyager US; Harper Perennial; HarperAcademic and Harper Audio.

10 53rd Street

New York, NY 10022

(212) 207-7000

harpercollins.com

Macmillan Publishers

Macmillan is a global trade publishing company, owned by the German Company Verlagsgruppe Georg von Holtzbrinck, with imprints in the United States, Germany, the United Kingdom, Australia, South Africa, and around the world.

The Macmillan U.S. trade book publishers include Farrar, Straus and Giroux; Henry Holt and Company; Picador; St. Martin's Press; Tor/Forge; Macmillan Audio; and Macmillan Children's Publishing Group. Macmillan also publishes into the college and academic book marketplace. In the many of the Macmillan U.S. publishers headquartered in New York City's historic Flatiron Building.

175 Fifth Avenue

New York, NY 10010

646-307-5151

us.macmillan.com

Penguin Random House

Originally international publishing giants in their own rights, on July 1, 2013, Penguin, a Pearson company and Random House, owned by the German company Bertelsmann, combined their adult and children's fiction and non-fiction print and digital trade book publishing divisions.

As a result, Penguin Random House has nearly 250 imprints and publishing houses. Some of the Penguin Random House publishing groups are: Random House Publishing Group, Knopf Doubleday Publishing Group; Crown Publishing Group; Penguin Group U.S.; Dorling Kindersley; Mass Market Paperbacks, Penguin Group U.S.; Random House Children's Books; Penguin Young Readers Group, U.S.

Random House Offices

1745 Broadway

New York, NY 10019

(212) 782-9000

Penguin Offices

375 Hudson Street

New York, NY 10014

(212) 366-2000

Dorling Kindersley

345 Hudson Street

New York, NY 10014

(646) 674-4000

penguinrandomhouse.com

Simon and Schuster

Simon & Schuster was founded in 1924 by Richard L. (Dick) Simon and M. Lincoln (Max) Schuster with a bestselling crossword puzzle book. At various times in its history, it has been owned by Marshall Field, Gulf + Western, and Viacom. Simon and Schuster is currently the publishing arm of the media company CBS Corporation, where its diverse offerings include books in the adult publishing, children's publishing, audiobooks and digital book arenas.

Simon and Schuster's publishing divisions and imprints include Atria, Folger Shakespeare Library, Free Press, Gallery Books, Howard Books, Pocket Books, Scribner, Simon & Schuster, Threshold Editions and Touchstone.

1230 Avenue of the Americas

New York, NY 10020

(212) 698-7000

simonandsch

uster.com

5 Steps to Creating an Effective Business Plan for Your Book

As your book and cover are being formatted and designed, take a moment (or two) to consider developing a business plan for your book.

By exploring the five following elements and how they relate to your book, you're putting yourself in a position to succeed.

Step 1: Market Research- Any solid marketing effort should begin with research- discovering publishing and distribution channels and costs, learning what other books will be in competition with yours. This foundation for your plan should involve as much data gathering and fact finding as you can do. Are there titles similar to yours already available? What can you do to differentiate yourself from them? Tailoring your efforts to the preferences of your readers will provide them with added value and incentive to purchase your book.

Step 2: Create a Mission Statement- Developing a powerful; purpose-driven mission statement for your business plan is essential to helping you keep your goals and objectives in mind. A mission statement is a clear and compelling summary of goals, intended to focus your efforts in a specific direction defined by three elements: the purpose of your work, what steps you are taking to achieve the purpose, and the motivating factors behind why you plan to achieve your purpose. Your mission statement should inspire you to remain committed to your purpose, so be specific in describing the actions you plan to take.

Step 3: Document Your Goals, and Create Objectives to Achieve Them- When you make goals, you choose a destination on a map; by creating objectives, you choose your route to this destination. By putting your goals on paper, you will be better able to create solutions to achieve them. Will the number of copies you plan to sell be affected by the size of your target audience? Will you need to invest in a wider variety of marketing initiatives to compete with the number of titles in your category?

Step 4: Determine Your Distribution Strategies- Most self-publishing companies provide distribution channels online, so consider special sales outlets beyond online and bookstores. If your book is specific to a town or state, consider targeting retailers in that area for distribution. Gift shops, airports, or even restaurants are often eager to stock books that relate to them specifically. To determine the best channels for your book, seek out places your target audience shops frequently and begin networking with managers and decision makers.

Step 5: Strategize Specific Promotional Tactics- It's important to think about how you will sell your book in advance of your publication date so you can take advantage of early sales. The momentum you build at the beginning of your promotional efforts will set the tone for future sales. As you form your business plan, determine how much time you can dedicate to each of the following areas: publicity, advertising, sales promotion, personal selling, and printed materials.

Example OF A Marketing Plan

1. Product Description

The entire marketing process is based on having a good book to sell. Was it well written and properly edited? Does the cover and page layout look professionally designed? Will you make it available as a printed book, an eBook, or both? Before you price your book or begin distributing or promoting it, describe what your book is about in 100 words or less. Think of it from your readers' points of view. How can your information help them reach their goals?

Identify books that are similar to yours, and describe how yours is different from and better than competitive titles. A good description may be started by completing this sentence: My book helps_____ who want _____ get _____. Then, add your competitive advantage.

Finally, develop a strong mission statement. Your mission statement is a one or two sentence description of why you wrote your book. Reading this regularly will help keep you focused and motivated. For example, a good mission statement for a book about finding a job would be "Help unemployed people develop their job search and networking skills in a supportive environment so they find a new, well-compensated career position quickly."

2. Author Biography

As an author, you are also selling yourself as a product, so it is important to start making the right brand impressions early. Think of who you know, and also about your background in terms of how it can help you sell more books. What makes you the expert on this topic? Where did you go to school? In what clubs and associations are you (or could you be) a member?

3. Target Readers

You cannot market to everybody, so think about who will buy your books. Who is the typical reader you had in mind when you wrote your book? Is the person male or female? In what age group would you categorize your reader? For example, if you are writing a book about preparing people for retirement, your target reader description might include people in these categories: Employed males and females, age 50 - 65, and middle to upper-middle income bracket.

Give consideration to increasing the font size in the page layout a point or two to help people with poor eyesight see it better. Learn more in Guide to Targeting an Audience.

4. Goals and Objectives

Write a specific statement of what you want to accomplish in the next year. Some of your goals may be hard to quantify, but do so where you can. Do you want more reviews? How many more? Do you want more media attention? How many print articles and broadcast appearances will you seek? How many books do you want to sell? How much money do you want to make? Be realistic in your estimation.

Part Two: Action Plan. Given your descriptions in Part One, what specific things must you do to reach your objectives? It is helpful to group these activities under three major topics: 1) How you will price your book, 2) Where you will sell it, and 3) How you will promote it. The sections below include examples to help you get started. Your actions will vary according to your own content and target readers.

1. Pricing Your Book. The price at which you will sell your book could determine your sales, profits, and opportunities for long-term growth. Your final choice will be determined by your costs, distribution method, and competitive prices. Be strategic in your decisions. Choose a lower-than-average price if you 1) intend to sell directly to target buyers rather than through a distribution network to retailers, 2) plan to limit your promotional expenditures, 3) want to make your book more competitive against other market options, or 4) seek a long-term profit potential. You might choose a higher-than-average price if your content will be quickly outdated or is highly specialized, or if you have little competition. Another consideration is the format in which you deliver your content. For example, eBooks are typically priced lower than printed books because of the lower production and distribution costs. Lower-priced eBooks also tend to attract more potential buyers.

2. Sales Outlet Options. Sales outlets will vary according to each individual title. Be sure to conduct research and think about where your content will

have the best sales opportunities when deciding what works best for your book. Some ideas for sales outlet options include:

a. Home Design Alternatives sells to stores such as Michaels, Lowe's, Menards, Sherwin Williams, Bed, Bath & Beyond, Macy's, and Sears.

b. Source Interlink markets entertainment products including magazines, books, and related items.

c. Some retail operations, such as Petco, require that sellers work through their retail sourcing company, Siennax.

d. If your content is appropriate for gift shops at national parks, try to distribute your books through Eastern National.

e. If your content is appropriate for science centers, zoos, and aquariums, try for distribution through Event Network.

f. Bookstores selling non-fiction online such as IncBookstore.com for business and financial books, or the National Small Business Network bookstore

g. Search for independent and niche book clubs. Some websites that provide lists of book clubs by interest area are BookClubDirectory.com, Book-clubs.com, BooksOnline.com, and FreeBookClubs.com

h. The National Directory of Catalogs is a fee-based directory featuring detailed information on more than 12,000 consumer and business-to-business catalogs.

3) Examples of non-retail buyers could include corporate buyers, schools, associations, clubs for entrepreneurs, government agencies, the military and home-based businesses. These opportunities require direct selling since there are no distributors that sell books to non-retail buyers. Find prospects through online searches after reviewing the following:

a. What companies could use the information in your books? For example, for a book about sales techniques, you may want to reach out to sales managers, career coaches, and networks of sales representatives. Find names of companies and contact information at Manta.com.

b. Check out Wikipedia for a list of network marketing companies

c. Every business, organization, and association has a NAICS (The North American Industry Classification System) code specific to its category. Create a list of prospect in your category by searching NAICS codes by keyword.

d. Could your book be used as a fundraising item? If so, consider contacting Extra Mile Marketing.

e. Look to government agencies as a potential customer. Find federal work-for-hire opportunities and learn how to locate and bid on them here. First, be sure to learn the rules, regulations, and standards that govern the federal procurement process. A comprehensive government contracting resource is Fedmarket.com, which includes weekly newsletters on GSA schedules, proposal writing, and federal sales.

f. What associations could use the information in your book? For example, for a book about how to communicate in writing, you may want to reach out to the International Association of Business Communicators. Find names of associations and contact information for each at Weddles.com. Find a comprehensive online directory of associations at AssociationExecs.com or through the Directory of Associations. Do you have a book for dads? Visit the National Center for Fathering.

g. Books on most non-fiction topics are popular in libraries and on military bases. You can reach libraries through Baker & Taylor and sell books through military exchanges such as AAFES.com.

h. What other organizations could use the information in your book? For example, if your book is targeted to executive women, you'd want to contact the National Association of Women Business Owners or the National Association of Female Executives. If you target small-business people, reach out to the International Council for Small Business.

3. Promotion Actions. How will you reach and tell your target buyers about your book so they can buy it? Use a variety of promotion tools as described below, and promote regularly. Prospective buyers may need to see or hear your message multiple times before it drives them to purchase your book. Also, choose the promotional techniques that are consistent with your personality. For example, if you are not comfortable

performing on television, deliver your message through radio, print, or the internet.

There are promotional tools to fit any budget. Most public relations actions are free or low cost, while advertising, trade shows, and sending direct mail packages are more expensive. Finally, there are even some promotional actions for which you could be paid, such as public speaking or conducting webinars. Find the best combination of those listed below that fit your target audience and your goals, personality, and budget.

1) Write a one-page press release, focusing on what makes you and your book unique and important to readers. Begin your press release with a simple statement or question (your hook) that will get the attention of the reader. Your hook is the key concept that makes you or your book unique and beneficial to your audience. Your press release should fit on one page, be double-spaced and written in a way that is interesting and informative to the recipient.

2) On what TV and radio shows could you be a guest? Choose shows that people in your target audience will listen to or watch. For example, target shows such as The Dave Ramsey Show.

3) What newspapers could review or write about your book, or to which you could you send articles? What newspapers does your target reader read?

4) What magazines could review or write about your book, or to which you could you send articles?

5) Who could review your book?

a. Pre-publication reviewers like Library Journal, School Library Journal, Booklist, and Bookpage

b. Media outlets and bloggers. For media reviewers, search Literary Marketplace and trade publications for those with an interest in your niche.

c. Post-publication reviewers such as Midwest Book Review, Computer Book Review, Education Review, Military Book Review

d. Paid reviewers such as ForeWord Clarion and Kirkus Indie

e. Seek niche reviewers for non-fiction books online, such as eSuccessBooks.com.

6) What award competitions would be right for your book? Examples include Axiom Business Book Awards, Small Business Book Awards and the National Business Book Award. Some associations sponsor award competitions, such as the Independent Book Publishers Association's Ben Franklin Awards.

7) Seek advance sales through corporate buyers or by conducting pre-publication promotion. Consider arranging a launch party.

8) Time the introduction of your book with special marketing periods (key dates, anniversaries, etc.) relevant to your title. Find examples of these at HolidayInsights.com.

9) Get testimonials and endorsements. Sometimes called "blurbs," these are statements by people attesting to the quality of writing and the value of the content in your book.

3.2 Internet Actions. In today's internet world, it's important to market your book online to reach the widest possible audience. Websites, blogs, social media, and online forums are all important channels for promotion and building your brand.

1) Consider purchasing the website address with your name or book title and build a website. Search for websites that you like and then go to Web.com or Wordpress for step-by-step instructions for creating your site.

2) Start blogging to build an audience and your personal brand. You can create your own blog for free at sites such as Wordpress.com or Blogger.com. Create an author page on Amazon.com, Facebook and

Twitter where you can highlight your current and future books and build your image as an expert. Also, join LinkedIn to network with like-minded people and prospects. Join groups relevant to your subject matter to start building awareness. Participate in the conversation, but don't overtly promote your title.

4) Join other online websites and forums relevant to your title. You can find them by searching for those about your topic.

5) Check out MeetUp.com to find relevant groups to network within your area.

6) A webring is a collection of websites organized around a specific theme. You can find a directory of webrings here.

7) Record a podcast or consider hosting a webinar on your topic. Visit BlogTalkRadio.com for instructions to do it yourself, or have them create it for you.

8) When internet users search for your book, you want your website to be the first one they find. SEO (Search Engine Optimization) helps the search engines, such as Google, Yahoo!, and Bing.

Personal Selling Actions. As an independent author, you aren't just selling your book - you're selling yourself. You might find in-person selling and networking beneficial for connecting with potential readers face-to-face.

1) In what bookstores or other retail outlets could you conduct an in-store event or book signing? Focus especially on local retailers and businesses, airport stores, high schools, and colleges.

2) Are there association meetings at which you could speak? Rotary clubs, Chambers of Commerce, schools, corporate outings, trade shows, and meeting planners seek speakers for their events and meetings. 3) Is your book appropriate for speaking events at educational institutions, or do you have the opportunity to provide training for a company's employees? Find a list of Toastmasters clubs for ideas.

4) Attend or exhibit at trade shows, conferences, or appropriate events

a. Book Expo America

b. Regional bookseller exhibits (Search the American Booksellers Association site)

c. Tradeshows where your buyers would attend (Search BizTradeShows.com)

d. Niche shows are excellent sources of leads, information, and possibly sales in a more targeted arena. The smaller, local and regional shows usually cost less than national shows, but the number of exhibitors is also smaller, since the cost is based on the number of people attending. Examples include the Natural Products Expo West, the Gourmet Housewares Show and Wine Expos

5) Throw a launch party, inviting local media, friends, family, and people in your target market. Have copies of your book available to sign, as well as print materials with your website and social media information. Get the emails of attendees to start building out a targeted email list.

3.4 Direct Marketing Actions. These give you targeted and personalized contact with potential buyers. You can reach many more people through a mail or email campaign than through personal calls. You may find that the U.S. Mail (letter or postcard) may deliver to more people than email with the likes of SPAM filters. In either case, your results will be better if you conduct tests before you send to an entire list. Test the creative offer, the timing and the list itself before sending your package. The package you send (or email) should include a cover letter, descriptive flyer, and some response mechanism (business reply card). Consider some of these direct marketing actions:

1) Send a postcard or letter and brochure to potential buyers. Visit DirectMail.com or InfoUSA.com for one-stop places to purchase a list or have them produce and mail your package for you..

2) Purchase the subscription list for magazines reaching your target buyers and mail to them. For example, if you want to reach homeowners, get the subscription list for a publication like Traditional Home Magazine. Are you targeting seniors?

3) Purchase opt-in email lists and send email blasts. For example, if you want to reach small business owners, purchase a list for a trade magazine targeted at small businesses.

4) Email marketing can be an inexpensive way to reach a wide audience quickly. Consider a company like Constant Contact, which sends out emails on your behalf.

5) Order bookmarks, stationery, and business cards to present a professional and consistent image among your target buyers.

3.5 Advertising Actions. Advertising can be costly, but some authors may choose to pay for ad placements in online and print channels relevant to their titles.

1) Advertise in local newspapers or on radio shows if appropriate. Offer to provide your content in exchange for free ad space. Contact the advertising departments of your target outlets directly to examine your options.

4. Evaluation. Every few months after you begin marketing your book, compare your actual sales results with your objectives. Are you on target to reach them? If not, what changes can you make to meet your goals?

For sales goals, create a simple Excel spreadsheet with your forecasted sales for any period in one column. Then, insert your actual sales figures and automatically calculate the difference. Have a line for retail sales, library sales, corporate sales, etc. to point out where your revenue may be below that which you projected.

Made in the USA
Middletown, DE
19 November 2022

15486272R00089